Sikhism: A Very Short Introduction

VERY SHORT INTRODUCTIONS are for anyone wanting a stimulating and accessible way in to a new subject. They are written by experts, and have been published in more than 25 languages worldwide.

The series began in 1995, and now represents a wide variety of topics in history, philosophy, religion, science, and the humanities. Over the next few years it will grow to a library of around 200 volumes – a Very Short Introduction to everything from ancient Egypt and Indian philosophy to conceptual art and cosmology.

Very Short Introductions available now:

ANARCHISM Colin Ward
ANCIENT EGYPT Ian Shaw
ANCIENT PHILOSOPHY
  Julia Annas
ANCIENT WARFARE
  Harry Sidebottom
THE ANGLO-SAXON AGE
  John Blair
ANIMAL RIGHTS David DeGrazia
ARCHAEOLOGY Paul Bahn
ARCHITECTURE
  Andrew Ballantyne
ARISTOTLE Jonathan Barnes
ART HISTORY Dana Arnold
ART THEORY Cynthia Freeland
THE HISTORY OF
  ASTRONOMY Michael Hoskin
ATHEISM Julian Baggini
AUGUSTINE Henry Chadwick
BARTHES Jonathan Culler
THE BIBLE John Riches
BRITISH POLITICS
  Anthony Wright
BUDDHA Michael Carrithers
BUDDHISM Damien Keown
BUDDHIST ETHICS Damien Keown
CAPITALISM James Fulcher
THE CELTS Barry Cunliffe
CHOICE THEORY
  Michael Allingham
CHRISTIAN ART Beth Williamson

CHRISTIANITY Linda Woodhead
CLASSICS Mary Beard and
  John Henderson
CLAUSEWITZ Michael Howard
THE COLD WAR Robert McMahon
CONSCIOUSNESS Susan Blackmore
CONTINENTAL PHILOSOPHY
  Simon Critchley
COSMOLOGY Peter Coles
CRYPTOGRAPHY
  Fred Piper and Sean Murphy
DADA AND SURREALISM
  David Hopkins
DARWIN Jonathan Howard
DEMOCRACY Bernard Crick
DESCARTES Tom Sorell
DINOSAURS David Norman
DREAMING J. Allan Hobson
DRUGS Leslie Iversen
THE EARTH Martin Redfern
EGYPTIAN MYTH
  Geraldine Pinch
EIGHTEENTH-CENTURY
  BRITAIN Paul Langford
THE ELEMENTS Philip Ball
EMOTION Dylan Evans
EMPIRE Stephen Howe
ENGELS Terrell Carver
ETHICS Simon Blackburn
THE EUROPEAN UNION
  John Pinder

Available soon:

For more information visit our web site
www.oup.co.uk/vsi/

Eleanor Nesbitt

SIKHISM

A Very Short Introduction

OXFORD
UNIVERSITY PRESS

OXFORD

UNIVERSITY PRESS

Great Clarendon Street, Oxford OX2 6DP

Oxford University Press is a department of the University of Oxford.
It furthers the University's objective of excellence in research, scholarship,
and education by publishing worldwide in

Oxford New York

Auckland Cape Town Dar es Salaam Hong Kong Karachi
Kuala Lumpur Madrid Melbourne Mexico City Nairobi
New Delhi Shanghai Taipei Toronto

With offices in

Argentina Austria Brazil Chile Czech Republic France Greece
Guatemala Hungary Italy Japan Poland Portugal Singapore
South Korea Switzerland Thailand Turkey Ukraine Vietnam

Oxford is a registered trade mark of Oxford University Press
in the UK and in certain other countries

Published in the United States
by Oxford University Press Inc., New York

British Library Cataloguing in Publication Data

Data available

Library of Congress Cataloging in Publication Data

Data available

ISBN 978-0-19-280601-7

9 10 8

Typeset by RefineCatch Ltd, Bungay, Suffolk
Printed in Great Britain by
Ashford Colour Press Ltd, Gosport, Hampshire

Contents

Acknowledgements

Over a period of thirty years' involvement with the Sikh tradition my debts are too numerous to record. Hew McLeod deserves a special mention for his unstinting generosity in patiently and meticulously responding to enquiries for more than twenty years. I thank him and another ever helpful adviser, Sewa Singh Kalsi, for their comments on this book. I am grateful to members of the online discussion group, Sikh Diaspora, and in particular to Pashaura Singh for his many wise and erudite contributions. Roger Ballard, Jerry Barrier, Joy Barrow, Owen Cole, Jeevan Singh Deol, Lou Fenech, Doris Jakobsh, Gopinder Kaur, Gurinder Singh Mann, Harjot Oberoi, Dharam Singh, Jatinder Singh, Nikky-Guninder Kaur Singh, Darshan Singh Tatla, and the late Piara Singh Sambhi are among those who have stimulated my thinking and provided illuminating detail over a number of years, and I owe a special debt to Pritam Singh, Shinder Singh Thandi, and colleagues in the Punjab Research Group and the *Journal of Punjab Studies* (formerly the *International Journal of Punjab Studies*). Inaccuracies are fewer as a result of Hugh Beattie's expert attention. Thanks to Marsha Filion at Oxford University Press for her expert pointers to overhauling the text, and to Alyson Lacewing, James Thompson, and Peter Butcher at RefineCatch Limited for bringing the book to completion. The responsibility for any errors is mine. If I have inadvertently failed to acknowledge any specific publications, please send the missing information in order that the omission may be put right.

Abbreviations

Extracts from the Sikh scripture Guru Granth Sahib are indicated by the letters 'AG', representing 'Adi Granth', the standard compilation of this text; 'DG' refers to the 'Dasam Granth', a volume attributed to the tenth Guru.

Quotations from the Adi Granth and the Dasam Granth are from, or influenced by, translations that are listed in Further Reading.

In accordance with convention in modern religious studies, BCE and CE are used in this book in preference to BC and AD.

List of illustrations

The publisher and the author apologize for any errors or omissions in the above list. If contacted they will be pleased to rectify these at the earliest opportunity.

Chapter 1
Introduction

Sikhism is sometimes described as the newest and smallest of the world's religions. Its media image is predominantly male, and reports often suggest that it is a religion preoccupied with swords and turbans. Personal contact with Sikhs usually impresses the outsider with energetic hospitality. The scriptures bring the reader to a poetic vision of ordered harmony and unity and a spiritual discipline.

This book's aim is to provide a rounded account of Sikhism in its many aspects. Sikhs have a strong sense of being a community with a history of struggle, and so the sequence of this Very Short Introduction will, in the main, be chronological. Each chapter sets historical developments in a wider context, which includes the overarching question – what does being a 'religion', let alone a 'world religion', mean?

Sikhism is often portrayed as a neat package consisting of a founder (Guru Nanak), a scripture (the Guru Granth Sahib), places of worship known as gurdwaras, and the requirement to show one's allegiance physically (by not cutting one's hair, for example). In what follows, at every stage of the Sikh story, the not so neat processes involved in emerging as a distinct religion will be evident. These include Sikhs' continually evolving sense of identity, often in relation to their Hindu neighbours. These processes are still underway and spark passionate debate.

The word 'Sikhism' suggests that the book's emphasis will be on a religious system – on the theological and ethical principles of Sikhs. But that would be to misrepresent the teachings and values that have arisen from and impacted upon a particular people. It would also pander to a discredited understanding of religion as an abstract, defined entity, rather than as a fluid tradition, pulsing with life and difficult to pin down.

Like 'Hinduism','Buddhism', and 'Jainism', 'Sikhism' is a Western word, coined not by Sikhs but by outsiders from a Christian, northern European background. Like these terms, 'Sikhism' became current during the period of British domination of India. The term 'Sikhism' is nowadays readily used by its 'followers', but is not totally satisfactory.

'Sikhism' is an extension of the word 'Sikh'. From the outset it should be pointed out that Westerners are accustomed to hearing this word pronounced in the same way as the English verb 'seek', as if it had what linguists call a long 'i', but in the original Punjabi the 'i' is short. 'Sikh' is correctly pronounced like 'sick', though with a final consonant more reminiscent of 'ch' in the Scottish word 'loch' than 'ck' in 'luck'. 'Sikh' means simply a learner or disciple, as the Punjabi verb *sikhna* means 'to learn'. Sikhs are disciples of the Guru.

People who identify themselves as Sikhs answer the question 'Who is a Sikh?' in different ways. One authoritative definition is:

any human being who faithfully believes in:

One immortal Being
Ten Gurus, from Guru Nanak to Guru Gobind Singh
The Guru Granth Sahib
The utterances and teachings of the ten Gurus and
The baptism bequeathed by the tenth Guru
and who does not owe allegiance to any other religion.

Sikhs refer to their religious path as 'Sikhi' and 'Gursikhi' as well as 'Gurmat' (the Gurus' doctrine). They refer to the Sikh community as a whole as the Panth.

Statistics

Census figures show that in India Sikhs number over 20 million, close to 2% of the population. In 1991 nearly 80% of India's Sikhs lived in Punjab, and this is the only state in which they form a majority (approximately 63% in 1991). The next highest concentration is in India's capital city, New Delhi, where figures are, at the time of writing, hotly contested.

There are now Sikh communities in many other countries, the largest being in the United Kingdom, where the 2001 census counted 336,000 Sikhs, that is about 0.6% of the total population. The next largest Sikh populations – in Canada and the United States of America – had not quite reached 300,000 at the time of writing. Sikhs tend to be locally concentrated – for instance, approximately half Canada's Sikhs live in British Columbia.

The meaning of 'Guru'

Sikh faith and teaching can only be understood in terms of the role of the Guru. The Sikh is the learner, the Guru is the teacher. Sikhs explain 'Guru' as a word that means 'remover of darkness'. Whereas the word 'guru' (lower case), traditionally used in India to refer to a respected teacher, particularly a spiritual teacher, has by extension become current in English for any expert, for Sikhs the Guru (always with a capital in the Roman alphabet) refers to each of a succession of ten spiritual guides, the founding fathers of the Sikh faith.

But the concept of Guru embraces more than the ten human Gurus. The *gurbani* ('utterance of the Guru') is embodied in the scriptures. Since the death of Guru Gobind Singh in 1708, these have been

3

consulted and venerated as a living guide, known as Guru Granth
Sahib. Guru is also a name for God, the divine preceptor, who was
Guru to the first human Guru, Guru Nanak. The Sikh word
'Vahiguru' for God, as well as God's title, Satguru (the 'True Guru'),
are further reminders of this.

A separate faith?

Now an important question: does this community of mainly
Punjabi followers of the Guru (human, divine, and embodied in
scripture) constitute a faith in its own right? If so, what are its
markers? Five views, variously voiced by scholars, preachers, and
activists, by Hindus, Sikhs, and outside observers, need to be taken
into account:

i)   Sikhism is a Hindu *sampradaya* (that is, movement led by a
     succession of gurus).
ii) Sikhism is a 'derived' religion, drawn from the Hindu tradition.
iii) Sikhism is a blend of the earlier religions of Hinduism and Islam.
iv) Sikhism is a distinct revelation.
v)   Sikhs are a 'separate nation'.

The basis of the present book is a sixth response:

vi) Sikhism has evolved into a separate religion in terms of Sikhs' self-
     definition, and because Sikhism has all the markers of a religion.
     These include a separate scripture and calendar, separate life-cycle
     rites, places of worship, and a sense of shared history. At the same
     time, in common with other faiths, Sikhism cannot be fully
     understood in isolation from its religious, social, and historical
     context.

This context has, for most of its history, been the geographical
region known as Punjab, together with the religious traditions of
Hinduism and Islam.

Hindu and Muslim context

The word 'Hindu' arose as a primarily geographical, rather than doctrinal, term. Persians and Greeks were the first to use this word for people living east of the Indus river. (Etymologically, 'Hindu', 'India', and 'Indus' are related.) Unsurprisingly, then, Hindu – or Indic – religious tradition is inclusive, and this tradition stretches back through the millennia BCE with no agreed starting point or 'founder'. As well as its strong connection with India, Hinduism's unity lies in Hindus' respect for ancient texts – notably the Vedas – and in the acceptance of certain key concepts, such as the cosmic law of cause and effect, *karma*.

The Hindu community consists of devotees of countless gurus. From time to time a new scripture is written and becomes the central teaching of a particular movement (a *sampradaya*, the name used in Indian languages for a succession of gurus and their followers). Many *sampradaya*s have a particular regional base, so that, for example, it would be as unlikely to find a Punjabi follower of the Swaminarayan branch of the Hindu tradition as to find a Gujarati Sikh. The gurus of a particular *sampradaya* teach their followers about ultimate reality, often concentrating on a personal God and the ways in which devotees may best express their relationship with God. The Sikh Gurus are clear candidates. But is 'Sikhism' a Hindu *sampradaya*?

The advocates of this view are, for the most part, Hindus, who point out that: the Gurus' names and families were all unmistakably Hindu, rather than Muslim; the teaching of the Guru Granth Sahib is continuous with (as well as critical of) earlier Hindu teaching; some central Hindu concepts, including *karma* and reincarnation, are taken for granted in Sikhism; and in the gurdwara preachers sometimes refer to stories from Hindu tradition during their homilies.

Most social convention is common to Punjabi Hindus and Sikhs.

Some Hindu families, mainly those living in urban areas, unproblematically include Sikhs and vice versa. Sikhs celebrate on Divali, the Hindu festival of lights, and many observe the annual bonding of brothers and sisters on the day of Rakhi (Raksha Bandhan). Not surprisingly, at the partition of India in 1947 into Pakistan and India, Sikhs from west of the new border fled with Hindus to India.

But the readiness of Hindus to argue in this way may simply demonstrate Hindus' inclusive attitude to religious faiths, above all those that have developed in India. Sikh writers point to the way in which, centuries earlier in India, the Buddha's teaching was absorbed into Hinduism, and they periodically rally Sikhs to withstand the danger of disappearing into Hindu society. In any discussion of the relationship of 'Sikhism' and 'Hinduism' as two religions, caution is necessary, especially as no firm line can be drawn between Hindu religion and Indic culture.

Nor is the relationship of Sikhism to Hinduism a straightforward parallel to Christianity's relationship to Judaism, as a 'daughter' faith. The facts that the Sikh faith is not a missionary religion, and that relatively few marriages have occurred outside the Punjabi community, have ensured a culturally closer linkage between Sikhs and Punjabi Hindus than that between Christians and Jews. The difference in dynamic in part results from the very different numerical relationship between 'parent' and 'daughter' in the two cases. In one case, the longer-established tradition, Hindus, massively outnumber their younger offspring, Sikhs, whereas in the second case, the situation is reversed, with Jews being far outnumbered by Christians. In terms of sacred texts, while the Hebrew Bible is honoured in Christian tradition as its 'Old Testament', the most ancient Hindu sacred texts have no such place in the Sikh canon.

In North India Muslims as well as Hindus have often been inspired by charismatic teachers. Many Muslims were attracted to Sufi saints who emphasized spiritual practices. Unlike the Hindu tradition, Islam originated outside India, with the revelation of the Qur'an to the Prophet Muhammad in the early 7th century CE. Muslim teaching stresses that Allah (God) is one and denounces the practice of making images of God and worshipping in front of them. In this and many other ways, Islam runs contrary to India's indigenous devotional practices. At the time of the Sikh Gurus political power in much of North India was in the hands of Muslims, following invasions by Muslim armies under a succession of dynasties. One result of Muslim domination was that many local families had converted to Islam.

The suggestion that Sikhism is a derivative in part from Islam is misleading. Certainly, Guru Nanak used Muslim as well as Hindu titles for God. Some commentators have detected Islamic influence in Guru Nanak's emphasis on 'monotheism', and others have suggested that the degree of honour shown to the holy book echoes the position of the Qur'an in Islam. But these are only speculations. Resonances between faiths are not evidence of a historical or causal relationship. With Christianity, too, a faith that the Sikh Gurus did not encounter, there are deep affinities, one being in the Sikh and Christian emphasis upon divine grace (in Punjabi *karam*, *prasad*, and *kirpa*).

To sum Sikhism up as a 'blend' of the two senior traditions of Hinduism and Islam is analogous to writing off English as a creole of Anglo Saxon and Norman French, rather than approaching it as a language in its own right. At the same time, treating it as a distinct language, rather than as a creole, is by no means to dispute the linguistic continuities. Neither the Gurus, nor their Sikhs, set about making a deliberate mix, any more than the speaker of what came to be called English mixed careful measures of words rooted in Latin and Germanic languages and then calculatingly coined new words.

The claims that Sikhism is a distinct revelation and that Sikhs are a separate nation are addressed in Chapter 8.

Being Punjabi

Sikhs' sense of community is not just a matter of interacting with, and feeling distinct from, the other major religious constituencies of North India. It also has strong regional roots. The family origins of almost all Sikhs, wherever in the world they now live, are in Punjab. Exceptions include the relatively small numbers of Western converts to Sikhism, most of whom live in the United States of America, and Sikhs with Afghan and Sindhi ancestry. (Sindh is the southern-most state of Pakistan.)

Punjab is the region to which the families of each of the ten Gurus also belonged, although their lives were not confined to Punjab: Guru Nanak's travels are believed to have taken him as far west as Baghdad and Mecca and as far south as Sri Lanka; and both the eighth and ninth Gurus' lives ended in Delhi; moreover, Guru Gobind Singh was born in Patna in the present Indian state of Bihar. Nevertheless, any exposition of 'Sikhism' that omits the significance of Punjab for Sikhs is incomplete, especially as Punjab has come to be regarded as the spiritual homeland for Sikhs everywhere.

To give an example from recent fieldwork in Coventry, UK: young Sikhs, almost all of whom were far more articulate in English than in Punjabi, and most of whom had never lived in Punjab, equated being Sikh with being Punjabi. They used the two terms interchangeably when naming their 'religion'. Most had little or no understanding that a Punjabi could be Muslim, Hindu, or Christian, Jain, or Buddhist. However little Punjabi language they could understand, let alone read or write, they knew that Punjabi was their language.

Punjab (or Panjab, as it is often written, especially by scholars) is the land of five (*panj*) waters (*ab*) – in fact the tributaries of the Indus. These are, from west to east, the rivers Jhelum, Chenab, Ravi, and Satluj (or Sutlej), and the Satluj's tributary, the river Beas.

1. **Map of Punjab, showing the undivided Punjab before 1947, its division between India and the new state of Pakistan, and the subdivision of India's post-Partition state of Punjab in 1966**

A contemporary map (Figure 1) shows the India/Pakistan border cutting through the land drained by these rivers, so that only the Beas now runs entirely on the Indian side of the border. The present Indian state of Punjab is a fraction of Punjab before 1947. This was the year when India gained independence from British imperial rule and was divided into India and Pakistan. Then, in 1966, India's already smaller portion of Punjab was further divided, this time according to the declared mother tongues of the population, into the majority Hindi-speaking states of Haryana and Himachal Pradesh, and the present-day Indian state of Punjab with a majority of Punjabi speakers, and so of Sikhs. This division was the result of concerted agitation by Sikhs, led by their politically astute leader, Sant Fateh Singh.

The Punjabi language, like the other tongues of North India, is described as Indo-European, and is a distant cousin of most modern European languages. The word *panj* itself, like the other numbers from one to ten, is an example. For philologists it is cognate with the Greek *pente* and German *fünf*, while *ab* is a distant relative of the Latin *aqua*. Nor is it a coincidence that *nam*, a key Sikh term for the divine reality, is so like the English word 'name', or that Panth closely resembles the English word 'path'. Another important Sikh word is *amrit*, the water used in initiation ceremonies: *a-mrit* (literally 'not-death'), is cognate, via Greek and Latin, with both 'ambrosia' and 'immortal'.

Like European languages, too, Punjabi bears traces of successive invasions and migrations, including the arrival of Greeks in the 4th century BCE. Words of Arabic and Persian origin testify to the centuries of penetration and domination by Muslim rulers and by armies from further west. The Gurus' words for 'God' include, as already noted, Islamic as well as Hindu designations – 'Allah' and 'Khudai' as well as 'Paramatma' and 'Ram'.

One word that Punjabis use for being Punjabi (that is, for Punjabi-ness) is *panjabiat*, a blend of language and humour and tastes in dress, cuisine, lifestyle, and the arts. One frequent joke that Sikhs make against themselves gives a flavour of *panjabiat*: Sikhs from India often remark that Sikhs have no culture other than agriculture. Despite several generations of migration from the villages of Punjab, many Sikhs still identify themselves as a rural, unsophisticated, farming people, in contrast to the more urban Hindu community.

Being Punjabi involves distinctive traditions in dress, cuisine, music, and dance, as well as an enthusiasm for harrowing 'Romeo and Juliet'-like love stories. Most famous of these is the tragic tale of Hir and Ranjha, as told by the 18th-century poet Waris Shah. *Bhangra*, the rousing drumming, melody, and acrobatic dance of Punjabi celebrations, has moved and mutated a long way from rural festivities. Yet, despite fusing with contemporary styles and tempos in Western popular music, *bhangra* is still inextricably Punjabi.

Key Punjabi values quickly become apparent to the outsider. Hospitality is one, honouring the guest with plentiful food and drink. Another value is *izzat*, which is often translated into English as 'honour' or as 'family pride'. Failure to show generous hospitality would be a cause for shame to the hosts and would be insulting to the guest. Above all, over the centuries, *izzat* has been tied up with the way in which female family members behave, or are perceived to behave. Gossip about a young woman's supposed misdemeanours, especially by associating with a man from the wrong family, brings shame on her relations, and can result in violence.

The fact that many Punjabi families continue to observe strong preferences, sanctioned by cultural tradition, in their selection or approval of sons- and daughters-in-law, might suggest a rigidly structured or compartmentalized society. There is, however, in terms of popular devotion, widespread fluidity. Shrines where healings are reputed to happen, or where supplications are likely to be heeded, draw pilgrims from a social mix in terms of both caste and religious allegiance. The devotees, and in some cases the holy places themselves, are by no means exclusively Sikh, Hindu, or Muslim.

It is within this dynamic context of a Punjabi culture, richly textured by its social history, that we need to set the term 'Sikhism' and to explore its content, connotations, and limitations. This book will explore the ways in which Sikhism (in the sense of the Gurus' teachings) converges with Punjabi cultural norms, which are caught up in processes of unprecedentedly rapid change, and the occasions when the Gurus' priorities pull in a different direction.

Chapter 2 introduces Guru Nanak and the first four of his successors. The focus of Chapter 3 is the Guru in the form of the scriptures. The main thrust of Chapter 4 is the contribution of Guru Gobind Singh, particularly in forming a community of committed Sikhs, the Khalsa, with its own uniform and code. Two interconnected processes run through Chapter 5, which reports the often turbulent history of Sikhs in India in the 19th and 20th centuries. These are the Panth's increasing interaction with the West – in particular the British Raj – and the successive struggles to make Sikhs and Sikhism unmistakably distinct from Hindus and Hinduism. During this period, thousands of Sikhs settled outside India, and this Sikh diaspora is the subject of Chapter 6. Two controversial themes, gender and caste, as well as Sikhism's relations with other faiths, are addressed in Chapter 7, and Chapter 8 goes on to look at other issues facing contemporary Sikhs.

Chapter 2
Guru Nanak and his first successors

Introduction

Figure 2 is a Sikh devotional picture showing the ten human Gurus and the volume of scripture in a unified composition. In Sikh belief all are physical embodiments of the same Guru. One Sikh analogy for Guru-ship is a flame that lights a succession of torches. Sikh religious pictures portray two figures more frequently and more prominently than the others. They are Guru Nanak, the first (human) Guru, and Guru Gobind Singh, the tenth. For day to day guidance Sikhs turn to the Guru Granth Sahib. Accordingly, Guru Nanak will predominate in this chapter, the Guru Granth Sahib in Chapter 3, and Guru Gobind Singh in Chapter 4. Theirs will be the strongest influence in the book as a whole, as it is in Sikhism.

Historical and religious context of the early Gurus

Guru Nanak's life span (1469–1539 CE) corresponds approximately to the German reformer Martin Luther's (1483–1546). In North India and northern Europe, respectively, each proclaimed religious insights and set in train what have proved to be enduring changes to the institutional profile of religion globally. Both criticized superstition, ritual, and priestcraft, and realized the need to communicate religious teaching through the vernacular rather than through an ancient sacred language. But pushing comparison further risks misrepresenting both of these reformers. Any

2. A popular 20th-century devotional representation of the Gurus: the ten human Gurus, Guru Nanak surrounded by (top left to bottom left) Guru Angad, Guru Amar Das, Guru Ram Das, Guru Arjan Dev; (top right to bottom right) Guru Hargobind, Guru Har Rai, Guru Har Krishan (the child Guru), Guru Tegh Bahadar, and (centre bottom) Guru Gobind Singh above the Guru Granth Sahib (the Guru as embodied in the scriptures)

understanding of their impact necessitates some knowledge of what preceded them, and of the situation into which they were born.

Whereas Martin Luther's Germany was Roman Catholic, owing allegiance to the Pope in Rome, Guru Nanak's Punjab was spiritually and culturally more diverse, and its largely Hindu population was subject to Muslim overlords. In fact, another useful chronological comparison is that between the lifetimes of the Sikh Gurus (1469–1708) and the reigns of the Mughal emperors of North India from Babur, who ruled North India from 1526, until Aurangzeb, who died in 1707 (just one year before the death of Guru Gobind Singh). The Gurus' lives were directly affected by the actions of their Muslim rulers.

For example, Guru Nanak alludes movingly to Babur's invasion in his compositions. Babur's successor, Humayun, is said to have consulted Guru Nanak's successor, Guru Angad. The emperor Akbar visited the third Guru, Amar Das, and is believed to have granted land on which the Harmandir Sahib in Amritsar was later constructed. Later emperors' and Gurus' interactions included the deaths of two Gurus (Guru Arjan, the fifth Guru, and Guru Tegh Bahadar, the ninth) and the imprisonment of a third (Guru Hargobind, the sixth Guru). At the same time, the Gurus' organization of their followers in some respects echoed the contemporary imperial system.

The spiritual and cultural diversity was not straightforwardly that of a Hindu majority and a (politically dominant) Muslim minority. Hindus and Muslims were themselves diverse. The Muslim contemporaries of Guru Nanak and his successors included Sufis (many from the line inspired by the Indian master Mu-in al-Din Muhammad Chishti), with their emphasis on personal experience of God. Guru Nanak's Hindu contemporaries, like their descendants today, in general expressed their devotion to Shiva, to Vishnu, and to Mataji (the Goddess) through acts of worship involving offerings. Worship focused too on natural phenomena –

the moon, sun, and rivers – and on appeasing unpleasant spirits. Families observed the appropriate rites to mark different stages in life or following a relative's death, and people went on pilgrimage, especially to the banks of the River Ganges. A high-caste minority, the Brahmins, gave instruction and conducted religious rites for their clients, for example investing high-caste boys with the sacred thread.

There were several outstanding individuals of whom Nanak would have been aware. One was the semi-mythical Gorakhnath, a master yogi, whose followers were the Naths. Naths performed austerities, often as hilltop recluses, and were believed to have supernatural powers. In a composition entitled 'Siddh Gost' Guru Nanak robustly denounced this escapism from society.

There were also the Sants, notably the poet-mystics Kabir, Namdev, and Ravidas. Both Kabir's and Ravidas's parents were low caste and both have significant numbers of followers in the 21st century. (The medieval Sants need to be firmly distinguished from those 20th- and 21st-century Sikhs, such as the politician Sant Fateh Singh, who have also been designated 'Sant' by their followers.) Although it is deceptively similar to the English word 'saint', as it is frequently translated, the word *sant* comes from a different root, from *sat* meaning 'truth'.

The medieval Sants belonged to the wider *bhakti* movement, with its emphasis on personal devotion to God, and so they are referred to by Sikhs as *bhagat*s. North Indian *bhakti* then, as now, usually identified God with Vishnu's incarnations (*avatar*) as Rama and Krishna. However, Ravidas, Namdev, and Kabir castigated temple worship and pilgrimage as meaningless distractions from attention to the formless (*nirgun*) God within the human heart. They proclaimed a way to *moksha* (liberation from the cycle of birth and death) through interior devotion, a way that Guru Nanak and his successors consistently endorsed. They also denounced preoccupation with caste status.

How do Sikhs today know about Guru Nanak?

From earliest infancy, Sikhs' first impression of Guru Nanak comes from colourful religious pictures. These hang in their homes and gurdwaras, and create and reinforce the sense of an elderly man of saintly, meditative persona. The paintings of Guru Nanak are most often reproductions of well-known portrayals by the Sikh artist Sobha Singh (1901–86). The artist's imagination is true to Sikh tradition and sentiment, but he had no depictions, or even verbal descriptions, dating from the Guru's lifetime to guide him. Another artist, Bhagat Singh, painted a picture of a haloed Guru Nanak seated cross-legged. Obeying a spiritual master's instruction to meditate upon the scriptures, Bhagat Singh had seen Guru Nanak manifest himself and had only then proceeded to paint his portrait.

This 20th-century account of the artist Bhagat Singh's experience raises questions for the serious enquirer into faith traditions: whose word do we accept and on what grounds? As enquirers, how do we weight individuals' 'religious experiences', a community's oral, written, and artistic tradition, and scholarly analysis of this tradition?

Turning from visual representation to verbal, one discovers that the Sikh scriptures contain no equivalent of the Christian gospels. But much-loved narratives of Guru Nanak's life do exist in the form of the *janam-sakhi*s. The British Library in London holds two richly illustrated original manuscripts – the Vilaitvali *janam-sakhi* and the more famous 'B40' *janam-sakhi*. The collections available for children consist of the better-known stories, often ones which make a moral point.

Janam means 'birth' and *sakhi* means 'witness', 'testimony', or 'evidence'. Each *janam-sakhi* offers a sequence of episodes: many are miraculous happenings, and they introduce passages from Guru Nanak's poetic compositions. One very popular example of the

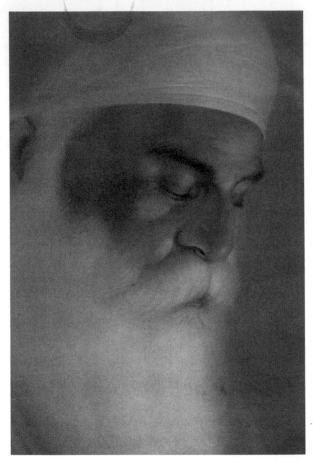

3. Widely reproduced portrayals by 20th-century artist Sobha Singh provide many contemporary Sikhs' image of Guru Nanak. This is his painting *My Meditation on Guru Nanak*, conveying the unity of Guru and Sikh in *nam simaran* (meditation)

supernatural element is the story of Guru Nanak's encounter with a poor carpenter, Bhai Lalo, and a wealthier individual, the revenue collector Malik Bhago, who – like Guru Nanak – belonged to the much higher Khatri caste. The *janam-sakhi* relates:

News spread through the village of Eminabad that the saintly personality, Guru Nanak, was staying with the low caste Lalo. Malik Bhago was hosting an impressive religious event for the benefit of his ancestors. Providing a feast for a large number of Brahmins, and presenting them with cows, were prominent features of the event, and Malik Bhago insisted on Guru Nanak's coming to the sumptuous spread. He asked the Guru why so distinguished a holy man had been eating with a low caste carpenter rather than dining with Khatris and Brahmins. In response Guru Nanak asked someone to bring some of Lalo's food to the house. When this arrived he held it in one hand, and grasped one of Malik Bhago's *puris* [deep-fried chapattis] in the other hand, and squeezed. Milk dripped out of Lalo's food and blood oozed from Bhago's. Guru Nanak explained that Lalo had earned his food through honest toil, while Bhago was trying to honour his ancestors with the proceeds of his extortion. He ordered him to pay for the cows that he had seized before making his offering to the Brahmins.

Leaving aside the historicity of such a feat, the story is one of many that suggest that the Guru, like the Hebrew prophets, used acted signs as a means of conveying moral points. In another *janam-sakhi* narrative, Nanak instructs a wealthy man to give him a needle when they meet after death. When the wealthy man protests that this is impossible, Guru Nanak points out the greater impossibility of carrying his riches with him.

Miracles always pose questions for the seeker after historical truth. Even though, for the most part, the supernatural happenings seem true to the thrust of Guru Nanak's hymns (for example, in the Bhai Lalo story, the importance of integrity and humaneness rather than of status or wealth), the idea that he performed such feats is at odds with Guru Nanak's stress on inward spirituality rather than outward display.

To the open-minded enquirer, the fact that each *janam-sakhi* episode ends in one of Guru Nanak's hymns suggests not so much that the incident concerned provided the actual historical context of the composition, but that during the centuries following the Guru's death his followers devotedly embedded his hymns in narrative – narrative that glorified their Guru.

In addition to the hagiographic *janam-sakhi*s, which are in prose, an early 17th-century *var* (praise poem) composed by Bhai Gurdas Bhalla also celebrates the Guru's life. Bhai Gurdas (1558–1637) is greatly respected by Sikhs: the title 'Bhai' (literally 'brother') is itself respectful. He describes how, at a time when Hindus and Muslims were 'selfish, jealous, proud, bigoted and violent', and unaware of the truth, the 'true Guru Nanak' appeared and 'the mist dispersed and light shone everywhere'.

It is, however, Guru Nanak's own compositions that offer the most authoritative understanding of the man himself, as well as of Sikhi. Bhai Gurdas knew these compositions (or *shabad*s) intimately, as it was he who later transcribed them to compile the volume of scripture at the request of the fifth Guru. But, if we look in Guru Nanak's hymns for history or autobiography we will be disappointed. Just four hymns (known collectively as the Babarvani, or utterances about Babur) refer to a contemporary event, in fact the terrifying and brutal invasion by Babur's army in the 1520s (AG 360, 417–8, 722–3). The focus of Guru Nanak's *shabad*s is not on temporal events, however overwhelming, but on divine truth and on attuning ourselves to this.

The *shabad*s convey a strong sense of an observant, sensitive, single-minded man, creative and iconoclastic. They are the words of a highly skilled communicator intent on helping others to transform their lives. The poetry teems with images of the countryside, of trade and industry, and of religious ritual:

> Make your mind the plough and your deeds the farming,
> Let your body be the field and steady work the watering.
> Let the Nam be the seed you plant. (AG 595)

and

> If my body were a vat and the crimson of the Nam
> Were poured into it,
> And if the dyer were my Master,
> Such a brilliant colour you would never have seen.   (AG 721)

Outline of Guru Nanak's life

The least controversial facts of Guru Nanak's life are these: he was
born in April 1469 (although his birthday is celebrated by Sikhs
everywhere in November) in a place now known as Nankana Sahib
in Pakistan. His parents, Mehta Kalu and Tripta, were from the
Khatri caste, which specialized in account-keeping. His older
sister's name was Nanaki. The siblings' similar names possibly
resulted from their having been born at their *nanake*, or maternal
grandparents' home. After his years of schooling, and his marriage
to Sulakhani, Nanak obtained a post as storekeeper for Daulat
Khan Lodi, the local Muslim governor, in Sultanpur. Sulakhani bore
two sons, Lakhmi Das and Siri Chand.

After some ten years in Sultanpur, when Nanak was about
30 years of age, he had the experience of being swept into God's
presence while taking his morning bath in the river. He then gave
away his possessions and devoted his time to spreading his
spiritual insights, principally by travelling extensively and singing
his poetic compositions to the accompaniment of his Muslim
companion, Mardana, who played the rebeck (a stringed
instrument). *Janam-sakhi*s tell how Guru Nanak's travels took
him as far as the Himalayas in the north and Assam in the east,
as well as to Mecca and Sri Lanka. On the western bank of the
Ravi river, at a place that he called Kartarpur ('Creatortown'
would be the best translation), Guru Nanak and his followers
formed a settled community that followed a daily discipline
combining work and worship. He composed 974 of the hymns
that make up the Guru Granth Sahib. Before his death in

1539, he appointed one of his disciples to succeed him as Guru.

Guru Nanak's message

'There is no Hindu, no Muslim' were Guru Nanak's first words after his river experience, words suggesting that religious labels are unhelpful and that no Hindus or Muslims truly follow their faiths. Both understandings are consistent with what he went on to preach. So, too, is the interpretation that true inner spirituality transcends the religions. When Guru Nanak refers to the specifics of the Hindu and Muslim religions, it is to provide the imagery for the spiritual path that he proclaims and, with gently probing humour, to show up religious hypocrisy.

Here is an example, evoking a Hindu mendicant:

> Let contentment be your yogi earrings;
> Let modesty be your pouch and begging bowl;
> Let meditation be the ashes you religiously wear;
> Let consciousness of death be your head-covering;
> Let pure living be your vow of celibacy
> And faith in God your staff.
> Accept all humans as your equals
> And let them be your only sect.   (AG 6)

The twelve words at the beginning of the Guru Granth Sahib are the most widely known by Sikhs. With the brevity of a text message, they sum up Guru Nanak's essential teaching. They also pose an immediate challenge to the translator. The twelve words are nouns and adjectives: they include no verbs or pronouns. To compound the challenge, the nouns have no exact counterpart in European languages, and the Gurmukhi script in which the scriptures are written does not have an upper/lower case distinction. As a result, the opening affirmation '*ik oankar*' can be rendered as 'There is one god', as 'One reality is', and 'This being is one'. Capitalizing 'God', 'Reality', or 'Being' affects the outcome in English. Is Guru Nanak making a monistic statement, that everything is one, and so appearances to the contrary – of, for example, God and creation being distinct – are illusory? Or is he voicing the monotheistic conviction that God is one and distinct? From the rest of this introduction to the Guru Granth Sahib, and from Guru Nanak's subsequent compositions, it is a monotheistic, rather than a monist, view of God which emerges.

But English renderings tend misleadingly to reinforce a Semitic understanding of monotheism, rather than Guru Nanak's mystical awareness of the one that is expressed through the many. However, what is not in doubt is the emphasis on 'one'. In the original, *ik* (one) is written not as a word but as a numeral, so emphasizing the singularity, uniqueness, and indivisibility of *oankar*. Similarly, *oankar* is represented as an alphabetic character, one nasalized vowel. The Guru's Hindu hearers already connected with the divine through *oankar*'s Sanskrit counterpart, *om*, that encapsulation of the universe's vibration in a single resonant syllable.

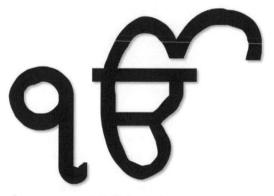

4. *Ik oankar*, a statement of belief and a logo, consisting of the Punjabi numeral *ik* (one) and the syllable *oan*, or the *oankar*, often translated as 'there is one God'

The remaining ten words are, in translation:

> truth by name, the creator, without fear, without hate, timeless in form, beyond birth, self existent, (known by) the grace of the Guru.

Many English versions convert this list of qualities to statements, often including a masculine pronoun or possessive adjective. The resultant sentences, starting with 'His name is truth' and 'He is the creator', immediately lend to Guru Nanak's words a masculine gender that is absent from the original.

Mul mantar is the name of these twelve words. A *mantar* (mantra) is an empowering formula for repetition; *mul* (pronounced to rhyme with English 'pool') means a root (it is etymologically akin to the *muli*, or white radish). It is as if the whole of the Guru's teaching (and of Sikh spirituality) grows from and draws sustenance from this statement. His longer compositions develop this theme, and provide the basis of Sikh theology.

Sikh theology

Truth is supreme and with this God is equated. The lines of the Japji Sahib which immediately follow the *mul mantar* emphasize this:

> Truth in the beginning
> Truth when time began
> Truth even now and for always

At the same time, God is the creator actively participating in the world. The creator-God does not, however, according to Guru Nanak, intervene in the world's affairs by means of incarnation. This marks a break with widespread Hindu beliefs about Lord Vishnu's interventions in the form of Rama, Krishna, and other *avatar*s. Nonetheless Ram, Mohan (a way of addressing Krishna), and Hari (the title 'Lord' often given by Hindus to Rama and

Krishna) recur in the hymns of Guru Nanak as ways of referring to the divine. So too do the Hindu names Shiv (Shiva), Braham (Brahma), and Paramatma (supreme soul), together with words from Islam for God – Allah, Rabb, Khuda, and Sahib.

For Guru Nanak this ultimate reality is *sagun* (possessing all attributes), as well as being *nirgun* (beyond all attributes). This paradox was not a new formulation, but the Guru's personal experience of what defies human expression that rings through his poetry. The divine is invisible (*alakh*) and formless (*nirankar*). God is also *niranjan* (literally, 'unsmudged with eyeliner'), that is, unentangled in illusion (*maya*).

Following immediately after the *mul mantar*, Guru Nanak's Japji celebrates cosmic order and divine will, a concept he called *hukam*. It is through the divine will that everything exists, and to *hukam* everyone should submit.

The *hukam* of creation reveals God, and so too does *shabad*, the word, in the sense of divine revelation, and *nam*, the name. *Nam* is central to Guru Nanak's teaching, as it means not only the word or utterance through which truth is revealed, but is itself the compression or encapsulation of divine reality. *Nam* is for Guru Nanak the total divine self-expression, rather than merely God's title or epithet, and on its power human life depends.

Guru Nanak communicates the immediacy of God through images, for example:

> You are the ocean, all-knowing, all-seeing.
> How can I, a fish, perceive your limits?
> Wherever I look, there you are.
> If I leave you I burst and die.

(AG 25)

Human endeavour

What Guru Nanak urges on his hearers is not so much a theological rationale as a constant spiritual practice, and not spiritual practice in isolation from life's ordinary activities and preoccupations, but as the grounding for these. So:

> Highest is truth but higher still is truthful action.
>
> (AG 62)

And this truthful action is rooted in continuous meditation, or *nam simaran* (remembrance of *nam*). *Nam japan*, repeating the *nam*, refers to the same practice, which is continued by Sikhs today as they listen to the singing of the Gurus' words in the gurdwara, on compact disc or via the internet, as well as when they repeat '*satnam*' ('whose name is truth') and 'Vahiguru' (which today means 'God', although in earlier times it meant 'praise to the Guru').

From Guru Nanak's verses it is clear that individuals face in one of two directions, either towards their *man* (pronounced to rhyme with the English word 'ton'), or towards their Guru. The *man* is our mind or psyche, especially in the sense of waywardness and capriciousness. The person who is *manmukh* (literally 'facing the *man*') is prey to *haumai* (self, ego) and to the five weaknesses of *kam* (lust), *krodh* (anger), *lobh* (craving), *moh* (materialism), and *ahankar* (pride). The more the *manmukh* yields to these, the further enmeshed that individual becomes in *maya* – delusion in the sense of wrong priorities, particularly of valuing the material over the spiritual. Guru Nanak's poem, quoted above, conjuring up the Hindu mendicant, concludes with '*manijitai jagu jitai*' (to conquer one's *man* is to conquer the world).

By contrast with the *manmukh*, the *gurmukh* is calm and focused, a pious person who dwells inwardly upon the *nam*. Guru Nanak describes meditation upon the *nam* as true worship (*puja*) (AG p. 489). But the *gurmukh*'s sustained practice of *nam simaran* does not mean escapism from human affairs. Unlike the Nath ascetics, the Sikh should not retreat to the solitude of the hills but must shoulder family responsibilities, 'trade in truth', and help others through acts of *seva* (voluntary service).

Guru Nanak's teachings point towards the equality of men and women and of all people regardless of their background. Chapter 7 will examine what Guru Nanak actually said on this matter, and how far 21st-century Sikhs enact his insights.

In his Japji, Guru Nanak maps out five stages of spiritual progression, commencing with the stage of *dharam* (duty) and peaking in *sach-khand* (literally 'the stage of truth'), that state of ultimate union between the individual *man* and God, a blissful, tranquil state beyond birth and death. This is *mukti* (the Punjabi and Hindi for *moksha*), meaning liberation from the cycle of birth after birth. The good news is that one can reach *mukti* before death. Guru Nanak did not challenge Hindu belief that the immortal soul or self passes through 8,400,000 lives before being born as a human being. He accepted the karmic law that we reap what we sow, with our deeds determining whether or how we will be born again, but he also stressed that human effort must be blessed by the grace of God and Guru. God's grace can transcend *karma*, and mindfulness of divine grace is a way of weakening ego.

Guru and *sadhsangat*

Guru Nanak stressed the need for a Guru. In the first instance, he most probably referred to God, the True Guru, as our inner guide, but Sikhs primarily understand his words as referring to himself and his successors. For Guru Nanak, the Guru is one's ferry across the ocean of existence:

> To reach Nam the Guru is ladder, boat and raft.
> The Guru is the ship to cross the ocean of the world.
> The Guru is place of pilgrimage and sacred stream.   (AG 17)

27

At the same time, the spiritual path must not be solitary. Like Kabir, Guru Nanak advocated associating with other followers of truth, the *sadhsangat*, or 'upright congregation'.

> The true believer, like the sandal tree, imparts fragrance to all.
>
> (AG 721)

His creation of a thriving community of families, sharing physical labour and religious devotion, shows how he grounded his preaching in well-organized practice.

Guru Nanak instructed his Sikhs to get up early, before dawn, to bathe, and then meditate during this *amrit vela* (ambrosial time). Guru Nanak's formulaic summary '*nam dan ishnan*' (meditate, give, bathe) adds the necessity of generosity (AG 942). Another more recent formulation commands Sikhs: '*nam japo, kirat karo, vand chhako*' (meditate, work, and share the proceeds). This threefold mnemonic is the basis of Sikh ethics. Life should be lived meditatively, industriously, and generously.

Nanak 2, 3, 4, and 5

Guru Nanak's successors are sometimes referred to as Nanak 2, Nanak 3, and so on, and they use the name 'Nanak', not their own names, in their compositions. Like Guru Nanak, his first four successors, Guru Angad Dev, Guru Amar Das, Guru Ram Das, and Guru Arjan Dev were all poets, whose compositions are to be found in the Guru Granth Sahib. Like Guru Nanak's, their hymns taught that *mukti*, often imagined as the soul's union with the Beloved, is the fruit of *nam simaran*, not of penance, pilgrimage, ritual, or caste observance. Chapter 3 will show the major part that these four Gurus also played in compiling the volume of scripture, and – in the case of the second Guru, Angad – in formalizing its distinctive script.

In institutional terms, it was probably the third Guru, Amar Das,

5. *Langar* is the key Sikh institution of preparing and distributing food and eating communally, with no concessions to rank. In India in November 2004, local Sikhs and Hindus participated in a *langar* in celebration of the 535th anniversary of Guru Nanak's birth

who gave prominence to the *langar*, a core feature of Sikh life. *Langar* is the provision and sharing of free food by all who come together for worship, and it makes a strong impression on everyone visiting a gurdwara for the first time. The word '*langar*' (meaning originally 'anchor') came into the Punjabi language from Persian, and a similar practice can be traced back several centuries before the Sikh Gurus to Sufis' resthouses which provided food for travellers – *langar*s continue to be a prominent feature of contemporary Sufi communities. No doubt sharing food together was integral to Sikh life in Guru Nanak's Kartarpur community and in the pilgrim resting places, or *dharamsala*s, which were the forerunners of today's gurdwaras. But it was Guru Amar Das who particularly emphasized the requirement for everyone to dine side by side, regardless of caste and rank.

According to tradition, when the Mughal emperor Akbar paid him a visit, he insisted that he too sit in line before joining the congregation.

So today, to sample characteristically Punjabi food, you have only to visit a gurdwara. In the *langar* you will be served with wheaten chapattis, thick brown *dal* (lentil soup), and, perhaps, spiced potato mixed with aubergine, plus a helping of plain yoghurt thickened with globules of chickpea batter, as well as sweet, milky rice pudding (*khir*).

In addition to emphasizing the importance of this 'free kitchen', Guru Amar Das established other practices that were more reminiscent of Hindu custom. He instructed his Sikhs to gather to worship the one God on the festival days of Vaisakhi and Divali, and he had a deep pool excavated at his home town of Goindval as a place of pilgrimage. Guru Nanak had used '*tirath*' (a ford or a waterside pilgrimage place) as a metaphor for contemplation of the *nam*; Guru Amar Das inaugurated a literal *tirath*. He also urged Sikhs to replace with hymns by the Gurus the Sanskrit verses that traditionally marked birth and death. His decision to specify times and places for Sikhs to gather comes as a surprise after Guru Nanak's dismissal of rites and pilgrimages in favour of inner spirituality. But it is just such processes of institutionalization that turn spiritual initiatives into religions and set them apart from other religions.

Reflecting the Mughal emperor Akbar's administration, Guru Amar Das divided the areas in which Sikhs lived into over twenty *manji*s (this word's original meaning is a string bed of the type that is still a familiar piece of furniture in Punjab), and he appointed preachers whose responsibility it was to lead the local congregations (*sangat*s). His successor and son-in-law Guru Ram Das further developed this administrative system by appointing for each *manji* a *masand*, a steward-cum-missionary, to organize the *sangat*'s worship and to collect its offerings. The requirement to give a tithe (*dasvandh*), to be used for the good of all, began with his son and successor, Guru Arjan Dev.

Guru Nanak's base had been Kartarpur, Guru Angad had lived at Khadur, and Guru Amar Das at Goindval. In their lifetime there was no settlement on the site of Amritsar, the city most strongly associated with the Panth today. But it was here, according to tradition, that Guru Amar Das decided to commence excavation of another pool, in a location already steeped in legend. Guru Ram Das founded nearby the settlement that came to be known first as Ramdaspur and later as Amritsar (literally, the 'pool of immortal water', or 'pool of nectar'). The excavation and building of a simple brick temple were brought to completion by Guru Arjan Dev. In this temple, in 1604, Guru Arjan installed the Adi Granth, the volume that embodied the powerful message of Guru Nanak and his fellow contributors.

Chapter 3
Guru Granth Sahib

Setting the scene

Every morning mobile phones and computers relay a passage of
Sikh scripture from the Harmandir Sahib in Amritsar. This is the
Guru's directive for the day. At 5.30 a.m. a *granthi* (attendant to the
Granth) opens the scripture at random, and reads the opening
words of the hymn at the top of the left-hand page. In this same
manner Sikhs everywhere seek daily guidance in their gurdwaras.
Such a message is called a *hukam-nama* (an order) or a *vak*
(saying), and a board in the gurdwara foyer displays the day's
guidance for everyone to read.

Users of English take for granted that a 'guide' can be either a
person or a book. But does the guidance provided by the Guru
Granth Sahib have the same relationship to Guru Nanak and
his successors as a guide(book) has to its author, or to a human
guide, or is the Granth a guide in some other, non-comparable
way? Sikhs believe that the volume, the Guru Granth Sahib,
is the last of the Gurus in the line from Guru Nanak. The sacred
volume is venerated by Sikhs as uniquely authoritative, and it is
absolutely central to their lives. Its physical presence brings a
sense of peace to the believer and requires a particular code of
behaviour.

The message of the Guru Granth Sahib

A single message shines through the Guru Granth Sahib, with song after song pouring out the soul's longing for God in compelling images. In their compositions Guru Nanak and his successors reiterate that to be free from the cycle of birth and rebirth depends not on caste or on performing the right rituals, nor will being an ascetic help. Instead, it is a matter of constantly meditating upon the *nam* in the midst of life's responsibilities and turning from one's ego towards God and Guru. The Granth's teaching crystallizes this certainty from the more multifarious emphases of India's religious repertoire. In the words of Guru Arjan:

> Of all religions the best religion,
> The purest deed, is repeating the Name of the Lord.
> Of all rites the holiest rite
> Is cleansing oneself of evil in the company of the saints:
> Of all efforts, the finest effort
> Is repeating the Name of the Lord forever;
> Of all speeches, the sweetest speech that transcends death is
> Hearing and voicing the Lord's glory;
> Of all places, the most sacred place,
> Nanak, is the heart in which the Lord dwells.

(AG 266)

How the scriptures were compiled

The first five Gurus played crucial roles in bringing the scriptures into being in terms of composing, transcribing, and compiling. According to tradition, when inspiration came to him, Guru Nanak would call Mardana and sing his hymns to the accompaniment of his rebeck. The likelihood is that written collections began during Guru Nanak's lifetime.

The third Guru, Amar Das, collected his own compositions into several books (*pothi*s), together with those of his two predecessors, plus compositions by the Sants Kabir, Namdev, and Ravidas, and by other like-minded poets whose verses chimed with theirs. These *pothi*s subsequently served Guru Amar Das's grandson, Guru Arjan, as a basis for the volume he was to authorize. Guru Arjan added hymns by his father, Guru Ram Das, as well as his own compositions, and Bhai Gurdas wrote out the text at the Guru's dictation. This was the volume Guru Arjan installed in Harmandir Sahib in Amritsar in 1604.

Today, the descendants of Guru Arjan, members of the Sodhi family, still live in a Punjabi city which bears the same name as Guru Nanak's settlement, Kartarpur. The Kartarpur *bir*, which they treasure, contains the text of that 1604 volume. The scripture that 21st-century Sikhs honour as the Guru Granth Sahib consists of the contents of the Kartarpur *bir* plus 59 hymns and 56 *salok*s (short verses, usually couplets) by the ninth Guru, Tegh Bahadur. One name given to this compilation, the accepted text of the Guru Granth Sahib as found in all gurdwaras, is 'Damdami *bir*'. The reason for this designation is the popular tradition that it was in Damdama in 1706 that Guru Gobind Singh dictated the entire text, from memory, to his companion, Bhai Mani Singh, after the Guru's hostile relatives had refused him access to the Kartarpur *bir*.

The Guru Granth Sahib is often referred to as the Adi Granth – hence the references to 'AG' in this book. '*Adi*' means first or original, and the designation distinguishes this compilation from a later anthology, attributed to the tenth Guru, which is known as the Dasam (tenth) Granth. Scholars also point out that Adi evokes the name of God as Adi Guru (the first Guru). The title 'Guru' denotes the volume's status, and 'Sahib' is a deferential term. As Sikhs show their respect for outstanding people, places of historic significance, and the scriptures by their ample use of honorifics, the full title currently in use is 'Adi Sri Guru Granth Sahibji', with 'Sri' and 'ji' further emphasizing Sikhs' veneration. In conversation Sikhs refer to the scriptures by a range of terms, including *bani* (utterance) and *gurubani* or *gurbani* (the Gurus' utterance).

The script

The script used throughout the Sikh scriptures is known as
Gurmukhi, usually translated as 'from the mouth of the Guru'. It
is the script of contemporary Punjabi, which has been since 1966
the official language of the Indian state of Punjab. Like the
scripts of all other Indian languages – except Urdu which uses
the Arabic alphabet – Gurmukhi runs from left to right. Unlike
the Roman alphabet as employed for English, Gurmukhi is a
phonetically consistent system – there is a one-to-one
relationship between its characters and the vowel and consonant
sounds of the language.

In 2004, the 500th anniversary of the birth of Guru Angad Dev
celebrated the second Guru's contribution to the Gurmukhi
alphabet. But widespread Sikh belief that it was Guru Angad who
formulated the 35-character alphabet does not take account of an
acrostic poem by Guru Nanak, based upon the Gurmukhi alphabet.
It appears very likely that Guru Angad formulated the script under
Guru Nanak's guidance, and that their starting point was a
simplified form of the older Devanagari script that was already in
use. As book-keepers and accountants, the Gurus' families,
including Guru Nanak himself during his years as a storekeeper,
were almost certainly using shorthand of this type. Although for
the first four centuries the words of each sentence were written
without spaces between them, today's Gurmukhi is spaced, so
making reading less of a challenge.

The language

Sikhs often explain that the text is in many languages – Persian,
Sanskrit, and so on. Such a statement can lead to
misapprehensions. Christopher Shackle, a linguistic authority, calls
the language of the Guru Granth Sahib simply 'the sacred language
of the Sikhs'. Even though the script throughout is Gurmukhi, the
vocabulary is very varied. Indeed, in one scholarly article, Shackle

translates one of Guru Arjan Dev's verses into medieval Latin and the second into Scots to point up the deliberate linguistic range within a single poet's repertoire. The basic language, which resembles contemporary Punjabi and Hindi, as well as the dialect known as Braj, is the inclusive poetic *lingua franca* of North Indian poet-mystics spanning the 13th century (when the earliest contributor, Farid, lived) to the 17th century. As the poets whose works were included in the Guru Granth Sahib came from as far apart as Punjab, Banaras, and Maharashtra, and as their religious backgrounds also differed, individual poets' stanzas show varying degrees of influence from evolving North Indian dialects and languages. These contained plenty of words from Arabic via Persian, as well as from India's ancient language of Sanskrit. The challenge today of reading a linguistically complex text of this antiquity must not obscure the Gurus' original intention of reaching a mass audience in the vernacular, rather than the small elite who could understand classical languages.

Format and structure

Increasingly, Sikhs read and hear the scriptures online, and the text is also published in sets of two or more volumes. But the greatest honour is reserved for the single volume of hard copy that is installed in gurdwaras. In the late 19th century, Christian missionaries in Punjab introduced the Gurmukhi typeface, primarily for the purpose of evangelism in Punjab by disseminating printed material in the local vernacular. In 1864, the first printed copy of the Adi Granth was made. Printed texts soon took over from handwritten ones and since the early 20th century the standard has been a 1,430-page volume. The page numbers that follow quotations from the scriptures in this book refer to this single volume.

The Guru Granth Sahib consists of poetic compositions and these are arranged primarily according to the musical mode in which they are to be sung. Within each musical mode these compositions are

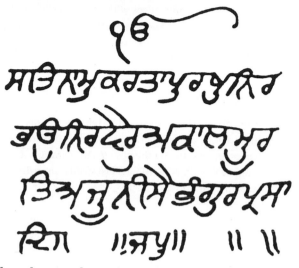

6. The *mul mantar*, the opening words of the Guru Granth Sahib, believed to be in Guru Arjan Dev's handwriting or to have been dictated by him, from the 17th-century volume at Kartarpur

organized first according to their length, from the shortest to the longest poetic forms. Within each genre, the poems are ordered according to the chronology of their writers.

Pages 1 to 13 consist of works that are used liturgically in morning prayer and in early and late evening prayer. These standard hymns contain a refrain. Pages 1,353–1,430 consist of miscellaneous compositions, concluding with a list of *rag*s. *Rag* (with a long 'a', like 'argue' in English) is the Punjabi form of the Sanskrit word *raga*, meaning the melodic sequence associated with particular moods and times of day. Like the Greek philosopher Plato, India's musicians have been in no doubt that music can induce changed states of mind. The 31 *rag*s represented in pages 14 to 1,352 of Sikh scripture include neither the saddest nor the most exuberant, but only those that evoke yearning, serenity, and joy.

Each *rag*-specific section commences with Guru Nanak's *mul mantar* and ends with what is known as *bhagat bani*, the words of the *bhagat*s, usually starting with works by Kabir and Namdev.

Sikh belief about the scriptures

It was, according to tradition, Guru Gobind Singh who declared that his death would be the end of the human line of Gurus, and that from then on the Panth and the *granth* (the community and the book) would be the Sikhs' Guru. His last words, according to his follower Bhai Nand Lal, were:

> Let anyone who wishes to see the Guru come and see the Guru. Whoever wishes to hear the Guru's word should wholeheartedly read the Granth or listen to the Granth being read.

In worship, as they repeat the conclusion of the Ardas, the congregational prayer, Sikhs affirm the scriptures as the 'Guru's body made manifest':

> From the Timeless One came the bidding
> By which the Panth was established.
> All Sikhs are commanded:
> Acknowledge as Guru the Granth
> Acknowledge the Granth as Guru,
> The manifest body of the Gurus.
> You whose heart is pure,
> Seek the Guru in the word.

On this basis, Sikhs' care for the scriptures takes into account human bodily responses to night and day. The belief, held by many Christians, that the elements of bread and wine are the body and blood of Christ offers a partial analogy for Sikhs' high regard for the Guru Granth Sahib as the Guru's body. The detailed veneration shown by Sikhs to the Guru Granth Sahib also helps us to understand why an occasional Sikh voice is raised to urge on all Sikhs the need to honour the content of the volume, by reading it with due receptivity, rather than solely worshipping its physical form.

Honouring the Guru Granth Sahib

The gurdwara (a word meaning originally 'doorway to the Guru') is a gurdwara only because it houses the Guru, in the form of the Guru Granth Sahib. The 1,430-page volume of Gurmukhi text spends the day reposing, covered by *rumalas* (brightly coloured covers made from velvety or satiny fabric) on a cushioned, canopied stand, the *palki* (literally, palanquin). If the volume is open, an attendant continually waves above it an item known as a *chaur*, a *chauri*, or a *chanwar*. Once you have seen a *chaur*, with its switch of fine, silvery hair (from a yak's or a horse's tail), mounted on a wooden or metal handle, you will recognize them in other contexts too. Paintings of Indian princes and Hindu deities often show one of the entourage waving one (or a fan of peacock tail feathers) above the dignitary. In Hindu temples you may spot a *chaur* among the items in a shrine. In India's hot climate, in the days before electric fans and air conditioning, keeping cool depended upon manual fanning, and on staying in the shade. Important people would certainly hold court under a canopy and have servants to keep the air in motion around them. The royal whisk or fan, and the canopy, came to signify authority – in much the same way as the Christian Church inherited the practice of burning incense from the court of the Roman emperors. It comes as no surprise that worship in the presence of the Guru Granth Sahib is called *divan*, the word for a royal court.

In the late evening the Guru Granth Sahib is ceremonially laid to rest (*sukhasan*) in another place: in many gurdwaras this is a small room leading off the hall in which the congregation gathers. In lieu of a *palki* there may be a bed. The name given to the room is, like the final stage of the spiritual journey as mapped out by Guru Nanak, *sach-khand*, the realm of truth.

7. A Sikh woman reads from the Guru Granth Sahib while another waves the *chaur*, as respect requires

These requirements mean that most Sikhs do not have a complete hard copy of the scriptures at home, as this means setting one room aside as a mini-gurdwara, with family members ensuring that the Guru Granth Sahib is opened in the morning and laid to rest for the night. Many more Sikhs keep at home copies of handbooks known as *gutka*. The most widely used *gutka* consists of the *nitnem*, passages used in daily prayer, which are a combination of liturgical passages from the Adi Granth and passages from the Dasam Granth. Increasingly, Sikhs hear the scriptures by playing audio tapes and compact discs, often at the start of the day, and via Punjabi television channels and the internet.

The sanctity of the bound scripture as a physical embodiment of the Guru also has implications for authorized printers of the text. Although most of the employees of the press in the basement of Gurdwara Ramsar in Amritsar are non-Sikhs, all undertake to abstain from alcohol and tobacco in accordance with Sikh discipline. After being printed the loose leaves are covered with *rumala*s, and any 'waste paper' is treated with reverence and duly cremated at Goindval in accordance with Sikh tradition. About 5,000 bound copies are published each year, and these are individually wrapped in a *rumala* and transported to gurdwaras in specially appointed luxury buses, or by aeroplane.

In April 2004, the *Toronto Star* reported how 149 volumes arrived at Pearson International Airport. Aboard the Russian-built Tupelov airliner each volume had occupied its own draped seat, before being carried on its own cushion, covered by a shawl, through the snow across the tarmac by barefoot volunteers to buses. From their special reserved seats the volumes were borne to a Sikh bookstore's specially built bedroom.

If a religious event is to occur at home, then a volume will be carried, wrapped in cloth, from the gurdwara. For the final few steps at least it will be borne on the bearer's head, while another person sprinkles water on the path ahead. The Guru Granth Sahib will then be installed reverently as described above, beneath a canopy. Moreover, only strictly vegetarian food is likely to be prepared and served during its sojourn in the house, and care will be taken by anyone on an upper floor not to walk directly above it.

On the subject of the honour shown to the Guru Granth Sahib, it is interesting to note that, a century ago during the period of British rule over India, the British officers of Indian regiments were required to salute the 'Granth Sahib', as Major A. G. Barstow's *Sikhs: A Handbook for the Indian Army* (1928) explains. By so doing, they recognized the power of the scriptures in maintaining the disciplined loyalty of Sikh soldiers.

Guru Granth Sahib in daily life

How central the scriptures are to the lives of Sikhs is readily evident if we consider the stages of the day. Of course, all who identify

8. On arrival in Toronto from Amritsar in April 2004, each of the 149 copies of the Guru Granth Sahib is carried on a Sikh's head, in the way reverence requires, to the waiting motorcade

9. A couple's marriage is solemnized by the bride and groom walking, linked by a cloth, four times around the Guru Granth Sahib, enthroned under its canopy. This photograph shows the Central Gurdwara in Shepherd's Bush, London. When the Central Gurdwara was opened on its earlier site in 1911, it was the UK's (and Europe's) first gurdwara

themselves as Sikhs are not equally observant, but few can be unaware of the scriptures' elevated position. For devout Sikhs, each day starts by bathing (between 3 and 6 a.m.) and singing or chanting Guru Nanak's Japji. In the early evening, Sodar Rahiras (a selection of nine compositions followed by five stanzas of Guru Amar Das's 'Anand' and two couplets by Guru Arjan) is recited, and the day ends with the selection of hymns (three by Guru Nanak, one by Guru Ram Das, and one by Guru Arjan) that are known as Sohila. Guru Nanak's long composition, the Asa di Var, is also favoured for early morning recitation. The morning and early evening recitations end with compositions by Guru Gobind Singh.

Holding a 48-hour unbroken reading (*akhand path*), a practice
which began 300 years ago, is a popular way of marking significant
occasions, including the commencement of a religious festival.
Most people assemble for the commencement and the culmination
of the reading. As it nears its conclusion, the congregation's mood
is one of anticipation and jubilation. Readers take their turn to read
in shifts throughout the 48 hours, and food is provided for all who
read or attend. Some families arrange for the *akhand path* to take
place in the gurdwara, others host the Guru Granth Sahib in their
home. In large gurdwaras several *akhand path*s may run
simultaneously. Individuals sometimes commit themselves to
reading the entire scripture, with breaks, over a much longer
period.

The scriptures are not only read but also sung. Sikhs do not talk
about 'services' but about *kirtan*, meaning collective singing of
the Gurus' *shabad*s. Often in the gurdwara the *sangat* listen as
*shabad*s are sung to the accompaniment of musical instruments.
These usually include the tabla (a pair of hand drums) and one or
two *baja*s (harmoniums), an instrument introduced to India by
Christian missionaries. Sometimes one musician plays a *saurangi*
(a relative of the violin). For percussion, a *chimta* (literally, 'fire
tongs'), inset with metals discs similar to those in tambourines,
is rattled loudly. By singing and by listening, all present are
steeped in the vibration of the Guru's utterance, the *gurbani*.
This means of remembering the divine name, of *nam simaran*,
involves one's whole being. *Kirtan* is holistic, aesthetic,
experiential rather than (primarily) cognitive, although
exposition of scripture often follows *kirtan*. It is an experience
of surrendering in devotion.

Worship ends with the *sangat* standing for the officiant's solemn
recitation of the Ardas followed by a *vak*. The *sangat* disperse after
the distribution of a doughy sweet, the *karah prashad*, which is
made from equal quantities of clarified butter, sugar, and
wheatflour, plus water.

Translation

Given the significance of the Guru Granth Sahib's physical presence, the fact that it is a work of poetry, and the key role of its musical expression, no adequate translation is possible. The discussion of Guru Nanak's *mul mantar* has already pointed up the difficulty of translating into English without gendering the language and introducing Judaeo-Christian overtones. In addition to the challenges of translating, there is strong Sikh resistance to the idea of using versions in English, or any other contemporary language, in worship. Nonetheless, English translations of the entire text and of selections have been appearing since the German missionary linguist Ernst Trumpp's unpopular rendering, which was published in 1877. Details of some subsequent translations are listed at the end of this book.

Other Sikh texts

The Guru Granth Sahib has unique authority among Sikh writings, which also include the Dasam Granth, a volume popularly attributed to the tenth Guru, and compiled by his companion, Bhai Mani Singh. But only a small portion of the Dasam Granth is familiar to most Sikhs, even though it occupies a more central place in the gurdwaras at Patna (in Bihar) and Nander (in Maharashtra), which mark respectively Guru Gobind Singh's birth and death. The Dasam Granth also figures prominently in the lives of two religious groups: the Namdharis (see Chapter 5) and the Nihangs (Sikhs who preserve 18th-century warrior traditions).

For 18th-century Sikhs, the Dasam Granth, like the Adi Granth, embodied the Guru, and John Malcolm, a British observer, reported early in the 19th century how it was placed next to the Adi Granth at meetings in Amritsar that made decisions in the name of the Guru. But, particularly during the 20th century, Sikh ambivalence towards the Dasam Granth increased with the realization that the Hindu stories it contains (and the stories of women of dubious character) challenged the view that Guru Gobind Singh was the sole author, or at least Guru Gobind Singh as conceived of by influential 19th-century reformers. There is still a tendency for judgements on what can be ascribed to Guru Gobind Singh to be driven less by textual analysis than by an 'orthodoxy' that dictates that Guru Gobind Singh could not have sounded like a Hindu worshipper of Durga.

However, Dasam Granth compositions over which no such question mark hangs are part of daily prayer and of the ceremony of initiation or commitment (the *amrit sanskar*, or *khande di pahul*). One of these, entitled Jap, is a rousing, rhyming invocation of God in 196 verses. Jap (rhyming with English 'harp') is recited each morning, following the Japji of Guru Nanak, as well as during the stirring of the sweetened water with which candidates are initiated. These lines (verses 20 and 80) give the feel of the whole work:

namo sarab khape. namo sarab thape.
namo sarab kale. namo sarab pale . . .
Salutations to the destroyer of all, to the creator of all.
Salutations to the killer of all, to the nurturer of all.

des aur na bhes jakar rup rekh na rag.
jattra tattra disa visa hue phaileo anurag.
With no particular country, dress, outward form or attachment;
Present everywhere, in all directions, all-pervasive love.

Other Dasam Granth compositions that are in liturgical use are those entitled Savayye, recited in the morning after Jap, and Chaupai, concluding the early evening prayers.

No other work is regarded by Sikhs as scripture, although works by two celebrated poets, Bhai Gurdas Bhalla (Guru Arjan Dev's amanuensis) and Bhai Nand Lal (Guru Gobind Singh's associate), are approved for recitation in gurdwaras. Preachers make frequent reference to stories from the *janam-sakhi*s, but the manuscripts corresponding to this oral tradition have no official approval for recitation. The *rahit-nama*s are the Panth's successive formulations of required conduct, but no *rahit-nama* has achieved canonical status, although the 20th-century *Sikh Rahit Maryada* (Code of Discipline) is an authoritative document of great significance within the Panth.

Chapter 4 highlights the non-literary aspects of Guru Gobind Singh's transformative impact on the Panth and the early evolution of codes of discipline. But it starts with Sikhs' best-known hallmark, the turban.

Chapter 4

Turban, Khalsa, and codes of conduct

Turban

'A *pag* plus a man equals a Sikh', a Sikh father explains to his son in *Goodness Gracious Me*, a UK television comedy series about British 'Asians'. (*Pag*, pronounced like the English word 'pug', is one of several Punjabi words for a turban.) A Sikh's turban usually consists of a length of fine cotton, tightly wound around the head. In 2004, a Sikh 'holy man' from Amritsar, who wound his turban from 400 metres of cloth, was hoping to be listed in the *Guinness Book of Records*, but the more usual length is between about 4 and 7 metres. Also in 2004, in New York, a Sikh police officer was dismissed because he refused to give up wearing his turban, and cab drivers in Long Island campaigned for the right to have their beards untrimmed and free-flowing. Indeed, one of the themes of Chapter 6 will be Sikhs' resistance to recurrent bans, not only on wearing the turban and being bearded but also on wearing a sword (a *kirpan*) in countries outside India. In their defence, the Sikhs concerned point out that wearing a turban is part of their religion, which forbids them to cut their hair or shave and requires them to carry a *kirpan*. The present chapter sets the turban and sword in historical context.

Turbans

Turbans come in many styles and colours, which often simply reflect individual sartorial preference. But the colour of a turban may express a political sympathy. For example, saffron was preferred by supporters of the campaign for an independent Sikh state. The colour may instead be customary for a particular occasion – for example, a man is likely to wear a pink, red, or orange turban for his own or his child's marriage ceremony.

Some turbans indicate the wearer's religious grouping. Evoking the tradition of 18th-century warriors, Nihangs (often called Nihang Singhs) tie towering dark blue turbans incorporating steel weaponry. The turbans of Namdharis (a group originating in the 19th century) are white and wound horizontally around the head in the style shown in pictures of Guru Nanak. The tall white turbans worn by some women show that they belong to an organization known as 3HO (see Chapter 6).

The masculine and martial 'Sikh look' should be seen in the context of Guru Gobind Singh's call, almost certainly in 1699, for conspicuous loyalty among his followers. In order to get to grips with a style of religious loyalty that is so visible, we need to look at critical confrontations during the 17th century, preceding the seminal event in 1699, and at the evolution of *rahit* (discipline) for his committed followers, the Khalsa, during the no less troubled 18th century.

At first sight, the concern with external indicators contrasts uneasily with Guru Nanak's dismissal of religious trappings in his

10. Nihang Singhs' dress includes a formidably high turban of dark blue cloth. This Nihang is raising his sword during a procession (March 2002) for the Hola Mohalla festival in Anandpur Sahib

insistence upon spiritual integrity. It needs to be stressed at the outset therefore that, from a Sikh perspective, successive Gurus acted appropriately for their time and consistently with a single spirit of Guru-ship.

The Five Ks

Generations of Sikhs and students of the Sikh religion learn that it was on Vaisakhi (often pronounced and spelt Baisakhi) 1699 that Guru Gobind Singh instructed his first initiates to adopt the 'Five Ks'. They learn too that these are the five outward signs required of a Sikh, and that they are called the 'Five Ks' because the Punjabi name for each item begins with the letter 'K' (*kakka* in Punjabi).

The Five Ks

These may be listed in any order. They are:

kesh (uncut hair)
kangha (comb)
kirpan (sword)
kachh (cotton breeches)
kara (steel or iron bangle)

It will be seen that the turban is not among the Five Ks; however, it is integral to male Khalsa Sikhs' expression of their commitment, and an insult to the turban is regarded by Sikhs as an insult to the Panth. In fact, as we will see, for one Sikh group, the Akhand Kirtani Jatha, the *keski* (a small black turban) is indeed on the list of Five Ks for both men and women in lieu of the *kesh* (which they also maintain; see Chapter 5). Such exceptions apart, the turban is regarded as a vital covering only for the *kesh* of male Sikhs since, in keeping with a tradition that extends from Iran to North India, this is the most honourable of male head coverings. Indeed, many more Sikhs wear a turban, and observe the injunction to avoid shortening their hair and beard, than undergo initiation. The turban has become synonymous with Sikhism, despite the fact that many men who identify themselves as Sikh are short-haired, clean-shaven, and turbanless, and despite the fact that, as some Sikhs realized for the first time in 2001, when the Western media were filled with images of turbaned Islamic militants, many Muslims also wear turbans.

11. The Five Ks which are required of all initiated (Khalsa) Sikhs. From left to right: *kachh* (cotton breeches), *kirpan* (sword, worn in a sheath), *kara* (steel or iron bangle), *kangha* (wooden comb), and *kesh* (uncut hair). In the photograph, the Sikh man is using his *kangha* to groom and then tie up his *kesh*

In religious terms, the long hair, carefully combed, neatly tied into a 'topknot' and then covered, represents disciplined holiness. The *kangha*, a small wooden comb, carries the same meaning and is to be worn under the turban. The *kachh*, which resembles loose-fitting white boxer shorts, represents sexual restraint. *Kachh* is spelt in various ways and Sikhs increasingly prefer the term *kachhahira* (also transliterated in a number of ways). Among the many meanings offered for the *kara* is that its circular shape is a reminder of infinity and so of God. Sometimes Sikhs describe it as a 'handcuff' to God, or explain that the sound of its chinking against their desk as they write is a reminder to use their hands only for good purposes. The *kirpan* represents the call to uphold justice and protect the weak. Sikhs sometimes link it to the word *kirpa* ('grace'), to underline the fact that it is not an offensive weapon. Certainly it should not be translated by the word 'dagger', which has unwelcome connotations of furtive dastardly assault.

Another way of understanding the Five Ks is to look enquiringly at their historical significance. Scholars have pointed to their close association with armed combat and to Punjabi assumptions about the body. In the case of the *kirpan* the military application is obvious. It is less apparent that the *kara* originated as protection for the sword arm as well as being usable as a weapon in its own right. In order to understand the practical advance represented by the *kachhahira*, one need only recall that it replaced customary clothing that was unstitched. *Lungi*s and *dhoti*s depend on being wrapped around the wearer's body and tied, and are thus not suited to energetic horse-riding.

But what about the *kesh*, which might seem less suitable for battle than a short back and sides? The suggestion of Hew McLeod, a distinguished New Zealand scholar of Sikhism, was that long hair was already the norm among members of the Jat caste who, by Guru Gobind Singh's time, constituted a substantial proportion of his followers. This suggestion was not well received by all Sikhs. Whereas long hair has been an essential element of female beauty throughout India, if a Hindu man's hair was uncut, it was usually because he had renounced the world to live as an ascetic with matted locks. The Sikh insistence on cleanliness, combing and tying the hair firmly in a knot, however, contrasts with the practice of Hindu renunciants, and the ban on hair-cutting rules out the far more widespread Hindu custom of *mundan* (head shaving) as a life-cycle rite for male infants. By maintaining their *kesh*, Sikhs affirm that the body, as divinely created, is sacrosanct in its completeness. (Biblically educated Sikhs gladly invoke the story of Samson, whose strength lay in his hair.) Together, the Five Ks are intended to distinguish Sikhs from both their Muslim and Hindu contemporaries.

For critical historians, an emerging issue is whether Guru Gobind Singh made the Five Ks a requirement for his first initiates on Vaisakhi 1699, or whether they evolved more gradually in response to social factors. Certainly, the Guru's announcement of the Five Ks is part of Max Arthur Macauliffe's account of events, published in 1909. But the earlier account by Joseph D. Cunningham, published in 1853, makes no mention of the Ks, although a 1915 edition includes them in an editorial footnote. Both these British scholars were strongly sympathetic to Sikh tradition. Hew McLeod's inspection of the manuscript sources led him to propose that the Five Ks were not formulated as a requirement until the late 19th century, when, as a result of the British ban on carrying weapons, an earlier requirement for Khalsa Sikhs to carry five weapons was replaced by the Five Ks. This analysis would be unacceptable to many Sikhs. Offering a middle path, Punjab's distinguished historian Professor Jagtar Singh Grewal's verdict is that:

> McLeod is right that explicit references to 5 Ks are rather late. But to assume that the 5 Ks were introduced in the eighteenth century is wrong ... The formulation came later but the substantive symbols were there from the time of instituting the Khalsa.

> (1998: 303)

The tradition of Vaisakhi 1699

The inauguration, or 'birthday', of the Khalsa is now celebrated by Sikhs worldwide annually on the 14 April – Vaisakhi day by the Nanakshahi calendar (see Chapter 8). As is the case on other major Sikh festivals, the Guru Granth Sahib is carried on a vehicle in a public procession, escorted by five men wearing orange and holding their swords upright in front of them. These five sword-bearers, the *panj piare* (literally 'five beloved ones') represent the first five Sikhs to volunteer their lives in the service of their Guru. Every Vaisakhi Sikh hears their heroic story.

12. *Panj piare* (five beloved ones) heading a *nagar kirtan* (procession through the streets with the Guru Granth Sahib) in Southall, UK, for the Vaisakhi festival. Each of the *panj piare* is carrying a *nishan sahib* (saffron pennant) bearing the *khanda* emblem

13. The *khanda* emblem

Vaisakhi had for centuries been celebrated on the first day of the Indian solar month of Vaisakh as the Spring harvest festival in Punjab. In 1699 Guru Gobind Singh (whose name until that day was 'Rai' not 'Singh') issued the order that his Sikhs should gather on Vaisakhi day at his headquarters in the hilltown of Anandpur ('town of bliss'). To the assembled crowd's amazement, the Guru emerged from his tent, brandishing his sword, and demanded the head of a loyal Sikh. One by one, five men, from a range of castes, volunteered. Their names were Daya Ram, Dharam Das, Himmat Rai, Sahib Chand, and Muhakam Chand. In turn, each disappeared into the Guru's tent and the horrified crowd saw blood trickle out. Then the Guru emerged, with the five men unscathed and identically clad. Some Sikh accounts suggest that the Guru had in fact slain five goats to achieve this effect in order to test his followers' courage and commitment to him. Generally Sikhs accept that a miracle took place, which should not be explained away.

What happened next was an initiation ceremony, on which Sikh initiation ceremonies ever since have been modelled. It replaced an earlier practice in which initiates had to drink water in which the Guru had dipped his foot. With a *khanda* (a double-edged sword) Guru Gobind stirred water in an iron bowl, and repeated over it verses, including Guru Nanak's Japji and his own Jap. Tradition has it that two sparrows drank some, flew away and fought to the death, so demonstrating the potency of the *amrit* (water of immortality) that he had prepared. At this point, the Guru's wife, at his request, added *patase* (sugar sweets) to the water. The implication is that initiated Sikhs, the Khalsa, will be warriors who are also able to live at peace.

The rite itself is referred to in Punjabi both as *khande di pahul* (initiation with the double-edged sword) and as *amrit sanskar* (*sanskar* means life-cycle rite). *Amrit chhakana* means to 'take *amrit*' or, in other words, to be initiated. The rite is also frequently called baptism. The exact procedure that the Guru carried out is the subject of some scholarly uncertainty, and present-day ceremonies differ from each other in some details. The following reconstruction is based on the continuing Sikh perception of what took place, and it concurs with the specification in the Sikh Rahit Maryada.

The Guru gave each of the *panj piare* in turn five palmfuls of the *amrit* to drink and sprinkled it five times in their eyes and on their hair. Each time, the recipient repeated '*Vahiguru ji ka khalsa, Vahiguruji ki fateh*'. These words, which Sikhs still use as an antiphonal greeting, mean that the Khalsa is God's and victory is God's. Guru Gobind Rai next received *amrit* from them in the same manner, and gave them and himself the name Singh ('lion') to replace their caste-specific names. It was at this juncture that, tradition has it, he instructed them, as his Khalsa, to adhere to the Five Ks and to observe certain rules and prohibitions.

Khalsa

The Khalsa must, the Guru insisted, be a casteless body of his Sikhs, outwardly distinguishable by the Five Ks, brave in battle, and ever ready to protect the defenceless. They must rise early, bathe, read the prescribed hymns of the Gurus, and meditate on the *nam*. They must not commit adultery with Muslim women (this evolved into a total ban on adultery), worship Hindu deities, or go on pilgrimage. Nor should they associate with the followers of individuals (in most cases the discomfited sons of Gurus) who had challenged the generally accepted succession of Gurus. The Guru's Sikhs must refrain from alcohol and tobacco (at that time smoked in a hookah), and avoid narcotics and halal meat. Sikhs who observed this discipline would be the Guru's Khalsa. He reassured them that: 'Wherever there are five Sikhs assembled who abide by the Guru's teaching, know that I am in the midst of them henceforth, the Guru is the Khalsa and the Khalsa is the Guru.'

Khalsa is a word of Arabic origin: *khalis* means 'pure'. As used in the contemporary Persian language of North India during the period of Mughal rule, *khalsa* meant land that was in the emperor's direct possession, as distinct from lands owned by his lords. The administrative innovations of earlier Gurus had resulted in a growing number of *masand*s (agents), but also in a decline in their integrity, as they ceased to forward Sikhs' increasing offerings to the Guru. Even before 1699, *khalsa* denoted groups of Sikhs whose loyalty was to the Guru rather than to intermediaries.

In his autobiographical poem, 'Bachitar Natak' (literally, 'wonderful drama'), Guru Gobind Singh leaves no doubt of his certainty of a divinely appointed mission to fulfil. At the time of his death in 1708, at the age of 42, he had not only been responsible for composing some or all of the Dasam Granth and for conferring Guru-ship upon the Adi Granth, which he had brought to completion by the addition of his father's compositions, but he had also transformed the Panth through his creation of the Khalsa.

Sword: martyrdom and militarization

Narrators of Sikh history usually report the transition of the Panth from the disciplined devotees of the 15th century to the fearless fighters of the 17th as a result of the *shahidi* (martyrdom) of two Gurus. According to this narrative, it was in response to their fathers' deaths at the hands of the ruling Mughals that the sixth Guru, Hargobind, and the tenth, Gobind Singh, took decisive steps towards arming the Sikhs.

During the 16th and 17th centuries, Sikhs were becoming an increasingly distinct community. Moreover, during the 17th century many Sikhs fought in battle and some suffered horrific deaths. Descriptions of courage on the battlefield and heroic death at the hands of political oppressors inspired and validated Sikhs' resistance movements during the 20th century, and their martial and martyr ideals are strong features of Sikhism. The *sant sipahi* (saint soldier, or holy warrior) provides a powerful inspiration, fusing the imperatives to be contemplative and vigilantly proactive.

Retelling the stories, though briefly, of the deaths of Guru Arjan and Guru Tegh Bahadar will give some idea of the rousing accounts that Sikh children hear from their elders, and which preachers and artists keep alive within the tradition.

In 1606, during the first year of Jahangir's reign, the first Sikh *shahid* (martyr), Guru Arjan, was killed by the Mughal authorities in Lahore. According to Sikh tradition he was roasted alive on a griddle. Guru Arjan had been arrested on suspicion of having supported the claim of Jahangir's son Khusro to succeed Akbar as Mughal emperor. Jahangir's version of events, the Tuzuk-i-Jahangiri, states that the emperor was irritated by the fact that this 'Hindu' had attracted some 'ignorant, stupid Muslims'.

Immediately following Guru Arjan's death, his son and successor,

Guru Hargobind, wore two swords for his investiture as Guru. One sword, he explained, stood for spiritual authority (*piri*) and the other for temporal power (*miri*). Subsequently, Guru Hargobind had a platform constructed opposite the Harmandir Sahib in Amritsar, as his headquarters as a temporal authority. This was the origin of the impressive building known as the Akal Takhat ('throne of the Timeless One'). The pair of Sikh pennants flying outside the Akal Takhat in Amritsar, and the two curved swords that form part of the emblem of the Khalsa, still remind Sikhs of *miri* and *piri*. In a further break with the style of his predecessors, Guru Hargobind instructed his followers to bear arms, and he led them to fight in four skirmishes with Mughal troops.

The second death that is regarded as pivotal in Sikh history occurred in 1675: Tegh Bahadar, the ninth Guru, one of Guru Hargobind's sons, was beheaded on the orders of the Mughal emperor Aurangzeb in Delhi, at the site of the present Sis Ganj gurdwara. According to Sikh tradition (which again differs from Muslim accounts), Guru Tegh Bahadar interceded on behalf of a group of high-caste Hindus, in fact Brahmins from Kashmir, who were being coerced to convert to Islam. The Guru declared himself ready, on their behalf, to offer his head rather than his faith. The word for 'head' is *sis* – hence the name of the Sis Ganj gurdwara. His three companions were brutally killed on the same day: Bhai Mati Das was sawn in half, Bhai Dial (Dayal) Das was boiled to death, and Bhai Sati Das was roasted alive in oil-soaked cloth.

Guru Tegh Bahadur's son, the future Guru Gobind Singh, had already begun learning the skills of warfare, and he subsequently led his men in armed combat with Hindu rajas in the Shivalik hills (to the east of Punjab) as well as with Mughal armies. Martyrdoms continued after the inauguration of the Khalsa in 1699: the Guru's four sons (ranging in age from 7 to 18 years) were all killed in 1705. The two youngest sons died in Sirhind, and visitors to the gurdwara there are still shown where the wall stood in which they were bricked up alive once they had refused to save their lives by accepting Islam.

Some Sikh *shahids* were fighters. Indeed, Baba Dip Singh (1682–1757), one of the most celebrated and most frequently pictured *shahids*, reputedly continued fighting, with his own head in his hands, even after receiving the fatal blow from his Afghan assailant.

Shahidi, the word which, since the 19th century, Sikhs have used for these brutal deaths, is in origin an Islamic word meaning 'witness', as it principally signifies deaths that bear witness to a noble cause, deaths that could have been avoided if the *shahid* (the martyr) had only accepted the option of denying the faith. The term *shahid* has come to mean, even more heroically, one whose death helps to overthrow oppression and replace it with justice.

For Sikhs, the 18th century was a century of armed resistance to oppression. Following the death of Guru Gobind Singh in 1708 at the hands of a Pathan in Nander (in present-day Maharashtra), his follower Banda Singh Bahadar rallied the Sikhs. While living as a hermit in Nander, he had become Guru Gobind Singh's 'slave' (*banda*). The Guru authorized him to punish persecutors of the Sikhs and a growing band of peasants followed him. They avenged their oppressors' violence against Sikhs by destroying the sites of their worst acts of cruelty including, in 1710, Sirhind. Banda Bahadar also struck his own coinage, symbol of a sovereign state. In 1716, Banda was captured, tortured, and executed in Delhi.

Warfare and decision-making

Formulations of distinct behaviour and appearance required of the Khalsa were compiled during the subsequent decades of recurrent conflict. After Banda's death, bands of locally based fighting men formed, which were known as *misals*. Their aim was to defend Punjab from its new enemy, the Afghan invaders of India. The

Afghan ruler, Ahmad Shah Abdali (also known as Durrani), invaded nine times from 1747 to 1769. In 1748, the 65 groups of fighters then operating in Punjab united into 12 *misal*s. During the Afghan invasions, the *misal*s became more effective and several combined into two particularly strong confederacies as the Bhangi *misal* and the Phulkian *misal*. When the Afghan threat ended in 1769, however, the *misal*s had degenerated into internecine strife before uniting under Ranjit Singh, the chieftain of the Shukerchakia *misal*.

The title of the *misal* chieftains was '*sardar*'; the more respectful form, *sardarji*, is the word Punjabis frequently use to refer to any bearded and turbaned male Sikh.

All the *misal*s would meet together, usually on the festivals of Vaisakhi and Divali. Together they constituted the Dal Khalsa (Khalsa army). When representatives gathered in front of the Akal Takhat in Amritsar, the assembly was known as Sarbat Khalsa, the whole Khalsa. Divali 1723 saw the first recorded meeting of the Sarbat Khalsa. Guru Gobind Singh's followers had divided into two factions, the Bandai Khalsa, who honoured Banda as their Guru, and the Tat Khalsa (Pure Khalsa), to whom this was unacceptable. On this occasion Bhai Mani Singh, the compiler of the Dasam Granth, successfully mediated between the two.

The decisions the Sarbat Khalsa reached were binding on the entire Khalsa. As they were arrived at in the presence of the Guru, in the form of an open copy of both the Adi Granth and the Dasam Granth, these decisions were called *gurmata* (the will of the Guru).

Evolution of a code of discipline

During the turbulent 18th century, a succession of documents were compiled, some in prose, others in verse, claiming to reproduce the injunctions of Guru Gobind Singh on Vaisakhi 1699. The *rahit-nama*s consisted of instructions for both individual and communal behaviour, and they provide a historical basis for the Sikh Rahit Maryada (Code of Discipline) that is currently in use.

One of these, the Tanakhah-nama, lists offences that incur the *tanakhah* (penalty of the Guru's displeasure). The lengthy list of proscriptions includes: not participating regularly in the *sangat*; giving a daughter or a sister in marriage for money; not paying one's *dasvandh* (tithe); not combing one's hair twice a day; adultery. Another, the Chaupa Singh Rahit-nama, has 800 or so prohibitions that include: female infanticide; drinking liquor; and failing to observe the following five requirements: *kachh, kesh, kirpan, bani,* and *sangat*. This last exemplifies the stages through which the present formulation of the Five Ks seems to have evolved and the relatively early formalization of the requirement for *kesh, kirpan,* and *kachh*.

In both their areas of consensus and divergence the relationship of the *rahit-nama*s to the actual exhortations of the Guru echoes the relationship of the *janam-sakhi*s with the life of Guru Nanak. Once again there is fertile soil for differing interpretations, including historians' deliberations over the order in which they evolved and over why some injunctions conflict with what is now regarded as approved Sikh teaching. Were 'purer' original versions 'adulterated', or are the versions which we have 'original', so providing clues for understanding the Panth's history subsequent to the 1699 event that they purport to report?

Vegetarianism?

The *rahit-nama*s also leave unresolved ethical issues, such as diet – vegetarianism versus non-vegetarianism – on which today's Sikhs disagree. On this particular subject, what emerges most clearly from the *rahit-nama*s is that *jhatka* meat (that is, from an animal killed with a single blow) is permissible. If taken together with the ban on intercourse with Muslim women and the command to avoid smoking (a habit particularly associated with Muslims in

18th-century India), the *rahit-namas*' guidance on meat-eating appears to be driven, in part at least, by a principle of maintaining social separation from Muslims rather than by considerations of cruelty or health, or for that matter of pollution, a Brahminical Hindu preoccupation. It is, rather, Sikhs' resistance to oppression and aggression by 17th-century Mughuls and 18th-century Afghans (in both cases Muslims) that provides the main key to understanding the Khalsa's martial character and appearance and the codes of discipline that took shape.

Diet offers an example of the *rahit-namas*' contribution to a subject on which Sikhs are divided. For many Sikhs it is unthinkable that an *amritdhari* (someone who has been initiated with *amrit*) should consume any non-vegetarian food, including eggs. But both the Adi Granth and traditional stories of the Gurus' lives are ambiguous. Guru Nanak's verses (AG 1289–90) pointed out that as humans we are caught up in the chain of life, that it is difficult to be completely free of exploitation, and that even plants are living organisms. His words were a response to the teaching of Hindu Brahmins that it is polluting to eat meat. There is a *janam-sakhi* account of Guru Nanak cooking venison to make a point and Guru Hargobind and Guru Gobind Singh are portrayed as hunting enthusiasts. Guru Nanak's words: 'The food that causes pain to the body and breeds evil in the mind is harmful' (AG 16), however, in the light of more recent knowledge, provide support for Sikhs who decide on being vegetarian.

As the *langar* is vegetarian everyone can partake in good conscience. In practice most Sikhs avoid beef in conformity with Hindu respect for the cow. The 20th-century Sikh Rahit Maryada is consistent with the *rahit-namas* in forbidding Sikhs to eat the flesh of animals slaughtered in the Islamic manner. But some Sikhs interpret this as permission to eat animals that have been killed by other methods while others understand the ruling as a total ban on all meat and so observe a strict lacto-vegetarian diet.

Through such debates, modern Sikhism has taken shape. Chapter 5 identifies the Panth's initiatives and tensions in the 19th and 20th centuries.

Chapter 5
The shaping of modern Sikhism

Introduction

Contemporary Sikhism is what it is because of a group of influential intellectuals and later political activists. The intellectuals are known by the 18th-century name of Tat (pure) Khalsa and they presented the Sikhi of their own and previous generations as sharply differentiated from Hinduism. The later campaigners for this cause are the Akalis, whose name 'deathless' revived that of fearless followers of Akal (God) in Guru Gobind Singh's time. This chapter starts by setting the Tat Khalsa in the context of 19th- and 20th-century Punjab, a period of competing Sikh reformist movements and the period during which key features of Sikhism took their present form, among them the Golden Temple and a distinctively Sikh marriage rite.

For nearly a hundred years (1849–1947), Punjab was ruled by the British, and the Raj's role in the ferment of modernization is an essential part of the narrative. As we shall see this included the challenges of Christian evangelism, the benefits of improved communication, the impact of legislation, the opportunities provided by the army, and the trauma and dislocation of Punjab's partition in 1947. Threading through this is a mounting consciousness among Sikhs of their identity. Expressions of this included the emergence of the Sikh political party, the Akali party, and campaigns (pre-1947) for control of their sacred sites and (post-1947) for a Punjabi-speaking state within India, as well as (in the 1980s and 1990s) unsuccessful demands for an independent Sikh state.

However, a uniform Tat Khalsa 'orthodoxy' did not totally win the day, and the chapter concludes with a variety of expressions of Sikh identity.

Maharaja Ranjit Singh's reign

The 19th century began with 40 years of Sikh sovereignty, the reign of Maharaja Ranjit Singh (1799 to 1839). After uniting all the warring *misal*s under his leadership he came to be celebrated by Sikhs as the ideal ruler, and the period of Sikh sovereignty is a source of collective Sikh pride. Maharaja Ranjit Singh (1780–1839) is acclaimed as Sher-e-Panjab (the Lion of Punjab), and remains one of the Panth's most popular figures. He received no formal education and smallpox deprived him of the sight in his left eye, but neither disadvantage held him back. He put an end to invasions from the West and held together a kingdom of over 100,000 square miles, stretching from the Khyber Pass to the Satluj river (at that time the frontier with British India) and from the north of Kashmir to the deserts of Sindh. Maharaja Ranjit Singh's style of Sikhi was inclusive, with Muslims and Hindus (and Europeans) playing active roles in his army and administration. He did not require his Muslim and Hindu consorts to become Sikhs, and his royal patronage embraced alike Hindu, Muslim, and Sikh shrines and celebrations. At the same time, coins issued during his reign were minted not in his name but in Guru Nanak's and Guru Gobind Singh's, so affirming that sovereignty belonged to the Khalsa.

The Golden Temple

Amritsar's Golden Temple is a reminder of the maharaja's patronage, as well as of Sikh resilience in previous centuries.

During the 17th century the sacred precincts had been repeatedly desecrated and the building destroyed. By 1776, the present structure, a harmonious blending of Mughal and Rajput (Islamic and Hindu) architectural styles, was complete. But the shrine only became golden thanks to Maharaja Ranjit Singh's patronage. His craftsmen faced the lower storeys with white marble and inlaid it with geometric, floral, and other designs in coloured stones including onyx, lapis lazuli, and carnelian. They beautified the interior walls with frescoes and elaborate decoration in mirror work and gold leaf. Gilded copper panels covered the exterior of the upper storeys, and these too were enhanced with pictures, inscriptions, and patterns.

Patwant Singh, an authoritative commentator, has written extensively on the history and architecture of the place Sikhs worldwide hold most dear. Of its unique significance for Sikhs, he writes:

> They came to it with untold wealth or a handful of flowers; to seek the blessings of the Gurus or in gratitude for blessings already received; to offer homage to the martyrs who gave their lives for this hallowed shrine, or to pray for the privilege of sacrificing their own lives for it . . . or they came for the sheer joy of seeing it calm and serene in the early morning light as they immersed themselves in the immortal pool.

> (1994, p. 154)

Religious fluidity and renewal

What is less well known is that during the 19th century some of the worship within the Golden Temple precincts was Hindu in style. Harjot Oberoi, a professor of history in Canada, has described the devotional plurality of 19th-century Sikh life. He uses the term 'Sanatan Sikh' tradition for the mix of religious influences and popular response. *Sanatan* means ancient and unchanging and is more generally applied to Hindu tradition, expressing its catholic,

14. The Harmandir Sahib, or Darbar Sahib, in Amritsar, known as the Golden Temple

all-embracing character. By no means all 19th-century Sikhs conformed to either 19th-century or present-day perceptions of Khalsa discipline. Instead, in keeping with the inclusive approach of their sovereign, many people revered Hindu scripture as well as the Adi Granth and Dasam Granth, their devotion to the Gurus extended to the Gurus' living descendants and to miracle-workers and ascetics, and they were comfortable with a range of shrines and styles of worship.

In this situation of an amorphous, undogmatic *sanatan* Sikhi two movements of renewal emerged, anticipating the Tat Khalsa's reformist zeal but differing from the Tat Khalsa in significant respects. Most controversially of all, both groups accepted the necessity of having a continuing line of Gurus.

The first group were the Nirankaris (not to be confused with the Sant Nirankari movement that began in the 20th century). The Nirankaris' founder, Dayal Das (1783–1855), was a contemporary of Maharaja Ranjit Singh. He called upon Sikhs to worship the formless God (Nirankar means formless, and was one of Guru Nanak's names for God), and to give up worshipping images of deities, patronising rites conducted by Brahmins, and going on pilgrimages. According to Nirankari tradition, it was Dayal Das, too, who began the distinctively Sikh marriage ceremony, in which the volume of scripture replaced the fire which is at the centre of the older Hindu rite.

The second group were the Namdharis. The name 'Namdhari' came from the movement's emphasis on the practice of repeating God's name (*nam*) – again a central strand of Guru Nanak's teaching. The Namdharis' ecstatic cries (*kuk* in Punjabi) gave rise to their other title, Kuka. Their founder was Balak Singh (1799–1862), succeeded by Ram Singh (b. 1816). Ram Singh's followers had to rise early, bathe, and then meditate using a white woollen rosary (with knots serving as beads). Their diet must be strictly vegetarian and their clothing simple, with men tying their turban of white cloth flat across the forehead. Marriages were to be inexpensive, but would be solemnized – like Hindu marriages – around a sacred fire, and the equality of men and women was emphasized.

For the Nirankaris, in addition to the ten Gurus from Guru Nanak to Guru Gobind Singh, there were Baba Dayal and his successors; the Namdharis, however, believed that their Gurus continued the line from Guru Gobind Singh without a break, as they held that he had not died in 1708 but had lived incognito for another century. Another difference between the two groups was their social

15. Sikh commander, Raja Sher Singh, leads his men into battle against the British in the second Anglo-Sikh War, 1848–9

constituency, with Nirankaris coming from the Khatri urban trading community and Namdharis belonging mainly to the carpenter caste.

British rule

In 1849, the British imposed their rule on Punjab's religiously diverse society and restored stability after ten years of bloodshed. They showed a romantic favouritism towards the Sikhs as a 'martial race', akin in physical prowess and ethical monotheism to Protestant Scottish clansmen. Given the Sikhs' resentment towards the British for overthrowing Sikh sovereignty, British enthusiasm for recruiting Sikhs to the army comes as a surprise. But Sikh soldiers had supported the British in 1857–8 in crushing a 'mutiny' by Hindu and Muslim soldiers. The outcome had long-term implications for the Panth as, in return for this loyalty, the British encouraged Khalsa tradition to continue in the army.

Indeed, service in the Sikh regiments, which were each attended by a padre-like *granthi*, required soldiers to conform to Khalsa discipline. Later, Major A. Barstow was to write in his *Handbook for the British Army*, published in 1928, that:

> Sikh soldiers, too, are required to adhere rigidly to Sikh customs and ceremonies and every effort has been made to preserve them from the contagion of Hinduism . . . Sikhs in the Indian Army have been studiously 'nationalised' or encouraged to regard themselves as a totally distinct and separate nation, their national pride has been fostered by every available means . . .

At the same time, the British administrators generally supported the increasing activity of Christian missionaries in Punjab. The schools which they set up introduced the risk of Christianity proving to be a more attractive option for young Sikhs than their own religion. Moreover, Christians had the lead in communications technology, as their printing presses commanded a far wider circulation than the Sikhs' hand-written literature. For many years the only Gurmukhi typefaces in India were those of the Christians' Ludhiana Mission Press.

Unsurprisingly, Sikh resistance to the erosion of their tradition began to surface. The Namdharis' leader, Guru Ram Singh, played a prominent part: decades before Mahatma Gandhi's more widely known movement of civil disobedience, Namdharis organized boycotts of British institutions. This included violence against butchers for dealing in beef – Namdharis were (and continue to be) passionate in their commitment to vegetarianism and in their reverence for cows. In 1872, the British government deported Ram Singh to Burma as a troublemaker and about fifty of his followers were put to death.

Like the Namdharis, the increasingly powerful Singh Sabha movement combined zeal for Sikh renewal with resistance to the British threat. (The word *singh* immediately connects with the tenth Guru and his Khalsa. *Sabha* means assembly – the two present-day houses of the Indian parliament are each known as a *sabha*.) It was from the Singh Sabha movement that the Tat Khalsa emerged. A growing number of educated Sikhs had become increasingly upset by the Hindu practices of the many *sanatan* Sikhs – in particular their patronage of Hindu ritual. The intellectuals who formed the Singh Sabha feared that this prevalent syncretistic tendency, together with Christian missionary activity, would fatally weaken the Panth. Firm counter-measures must be taken. They also disapproved of both the Nirankaris and the Namdharis because of their attachment to living Gurus. The foundation of the first Singh Sabha in Amritsar in 1873 was precipitated by the discovery that four Sikh pupils at the Amritsar Mission School had decided to be baptized as Christians. Another Sabha was set up six years later in Lahore, and other branches followed, all promoting what they saw as a return to pure Sikh values.

Soon a further stimulus to their efforts came from the newly founded Hindu reformist movement, the Arya Samaj, established in Punjab by Swami Dayanand Saraswati, a Gujarati. The rise of the Arya Samaj too can be attributed in part to anxieties about Christian incursion. After initially regarding the Samaj as their ally, the Singh Sabha Sikhs came to see it as a competitor, especially in its concerted effort to win over members of the most disadvantaged castes. When, in 1898 a learned Sikh, Kahn Singh Nabha (1861–1938), published an influential booklet with the title *Ham Hindu Nahin* (We are not Hindus), he did so in response to Arya Samajis' insistence that Sikhs were Hindus. In the prevailing mood of increasing competitiveness between Muslims and Hindus regarding the census returns for each comunity, one of the Arya Samajis' reasons for this assertion had been to boost the number of Hindus.

This was the period of a growing print culture. Like the internet a century later, printing presses meant that groups could disseminate their views more swiftly and extensively than ever before. In the process the competing groups' sense of distinctive identity intensified more strongly than in their spoken exchanges, because the circulation of propaganda by different communities in different scripts tapped into the emotive association between scripts and religious allegiance. Hindus identified with the Devanagari script, Muslims with the Arabic script, and Sikhs with the Gurmukhi script. (Devanagari, the script used for the Hindi language, links it immediately with the Sanskrit of the Hindus' ancient scriptures, while the Arabic script, used for Urdu, makes an immediate connection with Muslims' Arabic scriptures.)

What also became increasingly evident was that the Amritsar Singh Sabha was less insistent than its Lahore counterpart on an exclusively Khalsa-style Sikhi. Whereas the Amritsar Singh Sabha endorsed a wider definition of Sikhism, and accepted that *sanatan* Sikhs might well have much in common with Hindus without ceasing to be Sikhs, the Lahore Sabha advocated exclusively what they understood to be pure (*tat*) Khalsa values. The Amritsar Singh Sabha members' evident reverence for Guru Nanak's living descendant, Khem Singh Bedi, was certainly at variance with Tat Khalsa principles.

In addition to Christian missionary activity and the printing press, the impact of two other aspects of British rule upon the Panth fed into the competitiveness between communities: one was the ten-yearly census, requiring individuals to identify their caste and religious allegiance, and making Sikhs increasingly conscious of their minority status as compared to Hindus and Muslims. The other was the legal system. We shall see how, at the beginning of the 20th century, as Sikhs of Tat Khalsa convictions recognized a potential ally in the law, one piece of legislation hardened social differences between Sikhs and another helped to demarcate Sikhs from Hindus.

European writers

The printing press had already brought Sikhs and their religion to a European readership, and publications by British and other European observers are a part of the story of 19th-century Sikhi, documenting as they do developing understandings of the Panth's past. As early as 1790, Q. Crauford had alluded to 'the Seiks, a people who owe their religion to a Hindoo named Nanuck', and George Forster wrote of 'Nanock the founder of the Sicque nation' in his *A Journey from Bengal to England*, published in 1798.

One landmark publication was *A History of the Sikhs* (1849) by Joseph Davy Cunningham. So sympathetic was his account of the Sikhs that the British authorities transferred him from political service to regimental duties. Not only did angry British readers criticize his pro-Sikh position on the recent Anglo-Sikh war, but they accused him of preferring the Sikh religion to his own.

At the close of the 19th century, an Irishman, Max Arthur Macauliffe (1841–1913), resigned from his post as Divisional Judge in Punjab to produce a worthy translation of the Sikh scriptures. His remarkable contribution to Sikh studies – another landmark – was a six-volume work entitled *The Sikh Religion: Its Gurus, Sacred Writings and Authors*, published in 1909. His preface begins with the announcement:

> I bring from the East what is practically an unknown religion. The Sikhs are distinguished throughout the world as a great military people, but there is little known even to professional scholars regarding their religion. I have often been asked by educated persons in countries which I have visited, and even in India itself, what the Sikh religion was, and whether the Sikhs were Hindus, idolaters or Muhammadans.

Among Macauliffe's principal mentors was the scholar of Tat Khalsa

persuasion, Kahn Singh Nabha, whose crowning work was a
Punjabi encyclopaedia of Sikhism, published in 1931.

Akali movement

Sikhism in the 20th century shows the success of the Tat Khalsa in
defining Sikhism and the Sikhs as distinct from Hindu tradition
and community. But counter-currents ensured that ripples of
diversity have continued amid heated debate over who is, and who
is not, a Sikh. This was a century of struggles, both non-violent and
violent, for Sikhs' recognition as a faith community distinct from
the Hindu majority.

In 1902 a body called the Chief Khalsa Divan was set up with the
intention of bringing together the two wings of the Singh Sabha,
as represented by the groups based at Lahore and Amritsar. It
survived the temporary challenge presented by Teja Singh
(1867–1933), whose Tat Khalsa enthusiasm propelled him so far
that in 1908 he opened a girls' school to which pupils were (like
boys) required to wear a turban and he went on to issue his own
modification of the Sikh code of practice.

The Chief Khalsa Divan itself gave way to its radical, anti-British
element, which adopted the title of Akali. Sikhs' agitation began,
under British rule, as a campaign for control of Sikh holy places,
and it won Mahatma Gandhi's praise for its non-violence. In the
early phase of Sikh agitation, in the first quarter of the century, Sikh
activists' twin goals were establishing a distinctive marriage rite and
freeing the historically most important gurdwaras from their
hereditary custodians, who enjoyed their British rulers' backing as
the legal property-owners.

In their determination to show that Sikhs were not some form of
Hindu, members of the Singh Sabha resolved that Sikh marriage
should only be solemnized by the rite of Anand Karaj, the rite
already practised by the Nirankari movement. An Anand Karaj

marriage is solemnized by the couple sitting in front of the scriptures, hearing instructions on the duties of marriage, and then walking ceremonially clockwise four times around the Guru Granth Sahib. For these circumambulations the bride follows the groom, linked to him by a length of cloth. This takes place to the singing of Guru Ram Das's four stanzas evoking the progression of the individual towards union with God. The Anand Karaj achieved legal recognition in the 1909 Anand Marriage Act, a landmark in the recognition of Sikhs as a community distinct from Hindus.

Other life-cycle rites

It is likely that Sikhs' present naming and funeral ceremonies are also attributable to these early 20th-century reformers, with their Tat Khalsa aspirations for a Sikhi purged of Hindu practices. So, the religious procedure for selecting and conferring a name was not to be the Hindu method of choosing a name starting with an initial determined by an astrologer's reading of a horoscope. Instead parents would take the infant to the gurdwara. Here the *granthi* opens the Guru Granth Sahib at random, as if for taking a *vak*, and reads out the initial of the first word of the composition on the top of the left-hand page. The family concerned consult among themselves before deciding the chosen name. This the *granthi* then announces, followed by 'Singh' for a boy or 'Kaur' for a girl, as appropriate.

As regards funerals the Tat Khalsa reformers discouraged Hindu procedures such as placing the dying person on the ground or making a gift of cows and the deliberate exhibition of grief by beating the breasts and wailing. Instead, Sikhs are commended to turn to the Adi Granth for solace and guidance. The body, clad in clean clothes, is laid on the pyre and a *granthi* recites the Ardas for the deceased prior to the eldest son lighting the funeral pyre. As the body burns the late evening prayer (Sohila) is recited. Whereas Hindu Punjabis tend to take their relatives' ashes to Hardwar for final rites on the River Ganges, Sikhs go to their own sites, such as

Nander in Maharashtra, where Guru Gobind Singh expired or, more frequently, Kiratpur, the place where Guru Hargobind's ashes were scattered in the Satluj River. In the days following a death, it is customary for the scriptures to be read aloud in their entirety. Whether this is a continuous 48-hour reading or an intermittent reading over a period of seven or ten days will depend upon the wishes of the bereaved family.

As a result of similar Tat Khalsa concern, the initiation rite of *khande di pahul* (*amrit sanskar*), described in Chapter 4, was also defined in more detail than previously. This ceremony marks a step that is usually taken in adulthood, but sometimes by minors. The four cardinal prohibitions (the *kurahit*) were defined as: allowing one's hair to be cut; eating meat of animals killed according to Muslim rites; sexual intercourse outside marriage; and using tobacco.

Gurdwara management

Sixteen years after the Anand Marriage Act, another legal victory for the Akali campaigners was the Sikh Gurdwaras Act of 1925. It resulted from their protests centred on particular gurdwaras. It should be explained that these gurdwaras were now, by British law, the property of their guardians, the *mahant*s. The *mahant*s belonged to the Udasi order, whose origins went back to Guru Nanak's son, Siri Chand. During the 18th century, the Udasis' lack of Khalsa identity spared them persecution by Muslims. But it was this very lack of distinctness from Hindu society which was now an embarrassment as the *mahant*s drew no firm line between Sikh and Hindu practice. In fact, to the horror of the Sikh reformers, images of Hindu deities were worshipped in some gurdwaras. What was more, the *mahant*s were corrupt and the lifestyle of the *mahant* of the Nankana Sahib gurdwara, which marked the site of Guru Nanak's birthplace, was flagrantly immoral. British unwillingness to remove the *mahant*s stemmed from their interpretation of the situation as a conflict over property rights, whereas for the Akalis it was a religious issue.

By the terms of the 1925 Act, the custody of the historic gurdwaras of Punjab passed to elected committees, linked by the Shiromani Gurdwara Parbandhak Committee (Chief Gurdwara Management Committee), which is known as the SGPC for short. The SGPC could be elected only by individuals who were Sikh according to the Act's terms. The Akali movement's success in rallying Sikhs provided a basis for the growth of the Akali political party, the Akali Dal, and for its subsequent protest campaigns.

1947 Partition

Despite the mounting Indian opposition to British rule, in both 1914–18 and 1939–45 the Akalis supported the British war effort, at a cost of over 83,000 soldiers' lives and with over 109,000 wounded. But when India achieved its independence from British rule in 1947, Sikhs received no tangible acknowledgement of their

16. In World War I, Sikh soldiers in the Mesopotamia campaign march into battle behind the Guru Granth Sahib, held aloft

disproportionately great sacrifice. Instead, India was divided into two states, the secular state of India, with its massively Hindu majority, and the newly created Islamic state of Pakistan. Sikh negotiators had in 1940 and 1944 raised the possibility of having a separate Sikh state, but this cause was not pursued with passion until the 1980s. India's Partition was in fact the dissection of just two states, Punjab and Bengal. The cost was what a later generation calls 'ethnic cleansing', involving in Punjab alone the dislocation of some 12 million people – among them many Sikhs – and the deaths of another 500,000, as well as the loss to Pakistan of some 140 Sikh shrines. The one gain for Sikhs – and it was considerable – was that they were more geographically concentrated than they had ever been in the undivided Punjab. The Akalis realized the opportunity this presented for protecting Sikhs' religious and cultural traditions as well as the Punjabi language.

Ardas and Sikh Rahit Maryada

The loss of their historic shrines left its mark on the Sikhs' petition, the Ardas, which is recited at the close of congregational worship. It needs to be explained that the Ardas (from the Persian word *'arz-dasht*, a written petition) is the formal prayer which one person recites on behalf of the whole *sangat*. The leader stands in front of the congregation, like them facing the Guru Granth Sahib, and at certain points they intone the word 'Vahiguru'. Earlier in the 20th century Tat Khalsa scholars had finalized the second part of the text which summarizes the Panth's historical suffering and success. Now a line praying for access to the lost shrines was added.

To find the Ardas one need only look in one of the 20th century's classic reformist Sikh publications, the Sikh Rahit Maryada. This was published in 1950 by the SGPC and is the last in the line of *rahit-nama*s. It contains instructions for *nitnem* (daily prayer) and the Ardas and for respectful behaviour towards the Adi Granth and within the gurdwara, including *kirtan*, *path*, preparation of *karah* *parsad* and exposition of scripture. It lists prohibitions (*kurahits*) and provides details of the rites marking birth, naming, marriage and death. Sikhs are exhorted to provide *seva* (voluntary service), for example by serving the *langar*. Regulations for the *khande di pahul* rite precede information about *tanakhah* (penance) and *gurmata* (religious decision).

1966: redrawing the map

Although since 1947 Sikhs in the Indian state of Punjab had been more demographically concentrated than previously, until 1966 they formed a majority only in six districts. So, under Akali leadership Sikhs campaigned for a new state of Punjabi-speakers to be carved out, on the language principle of the Indian government. According to this principle, Bengal's boundaries corresponded to the area in which the majority were Bengali-speakers, Gujarat's to the area of Gujarati-speakers, and so on. What the Sikhs' political leader, Sant Fatch Singh, in fact sought to achieve was the first and only state to have a Sikh majority. In consequence, in the 1951 and 1961 censuses, Punjabi-speaking Hindus tried to thwart this campaign by registering Hindi as their language. But in 1966, the central government rewarded the Sikhs for their contribution to the Indian cause in the 1965 Indo-Pakistan conflict by redrawing the boundary of Punjab.

Jarnail Singh Bhindranwale and 1984

By the 1980s, some Sikhs had in their sights a more radical redrawing of the map, to create an autonomous Sikh homeland for the 'Sikh nation'. In the context of the unrest of the 1980s, a key figure was Jarnail Singh Bhindranwale (1947–84), the charismatic leader of the Damdami Taksal. The Taksal (literally, 'mint') was a centre of traditional Sikh study, teaching correct enunciation of the Guru Granth Sahib. Damdami Taksal issued its own manual of Khalsa discipline and has its own distinctive way of conducting the *khande di pahul*. One of the Taksal's earliest students was the noted

18th-century martyr Baba Dip Singh. Jarnail Singh Bhindranwale, usually referred to with the title of 'Sant', saw himself in this noble martyr tradition.

In addition to the collision course between his convictions as a traditionally trained Khalsa Sikh, ready to die as a *shahid*, and the pressures and enticements of modernity that were gaining ground in Punjab, he fitted the political situation. Indeed, he had initially been brought to prominence by Sanjay Gandhi, the second son of India's prime minister, Indira Gandhi. The Congress Party's political intention was to divide the majority of Sikh voters in Punjab who did not support the Congress Party. This was at a time when Sikh agriculturalists, most of them from the Jat caste to which the majority of the Sikh community belong, felt increasingly alienated by the prevarication of the Indian government which had not met its demands as listed in the Anandpur Sahib Resolution.

The demands of this resolution had originally been proposed by the Akali Dal in 1973; one was for a fairer distribution of canal water and another was for the city of Chandigarh, which is still shared with the adjacent state of Haryana, to become the capital of Punjab alone. Although the demands were more economic than religious, discontented Sikhs readily identified the Union government as largely Hindu (and so anti-Sikh). The Congress Party, which was out of office, needed a personality who would divide the Sikh electorate in Punjab, and Jarnail Singh was their man.

Few readers of George Orwell's novel *Nineteen Eighty-four* realize the disastrous connotations of the date for the Panth. In Punjab, violence was escalating, in a campaign for a separate Sikh state to be known as Khalistan, Land of the Khalsa, Land of the Pure. The killing reached a climax on the day of the annual commemoration of the *shahidi* of Guru Arjan in early June. When the hallowed precincts of Harmandir Sahib were thronged with pilgrims, the

Indian Government sent in its men and tanks in Operation Bluestar to remove Jarnail Singh Bhindranwale who had moved in during 1982. In the bloodshed, hundreds, and almost certainly thousands, including Jarnail Singh Bhindranwale himself, were killed. The Sikh Reference Library of historic treasures, including the Chaupa Singh Rahit-nama and manuscripts bearing the Gurus' signatures, was destroyed and the damage to the Akal Takhat meant that it too had to be demolished. Although the Government subsequently rebuilt it, Sikhs were so outraged that they razed this building and replaced it with their own.

Before the year's end, on 31 October, two Sikh bodyguards killed Mrs Indira Gandhi. And, in the resultant carnage, Sikhs were systematically attacked and murdered in Delhi in their thousands. At the time of writing, despite the publication of detailed reports, justice has not been seen to be done – although relations between Sikhs and Hindus have eased. In the absence of competent leadership, the ensuing violence in Punjab petered out in the mid-1990s.

Different emphases within the Panth

The life of Bhagat Puran Singh (1904–92) exemplified a very different expression of Sikhi from Jarnail Singh's. He dedicated his life to caring for the destitute and disabled, and the Pingalwara (home for the 'handicapped'), a complex situated near Amritsar's bus terminus, carries on his mission of compassionate *seva*, under its Patron President, Dr Indarjit Kaur. The All-India Pingalwara Charitable Society, employing over 400 people, resulted from Bhagat Puran Singh's decades of tireless effort for the abandoned, terminally ill, and mentally challenged. This began with his devotion to the helpless Piara Singh, whom he had found as an abandoned, dumb four-year-old, physically deformed and mentally impaired. Puran Singh washed and tended him, gave him the name 'Piara', meaning beloved, and for years carried him on his back as a 'garland round my neck'. Unusually among his contemporaries, Bhagat

Puran Singh was also committed to animal welfare, and to combating pollution of the environment. Sadly, his concern has not yet won strong support, although a Chair at Guru Nanak Dev University in Amritsar is to be named in his memory.

In parallel with the Akalis' and others' political struggle, the 20th century saw the emergence of several other Sikh groups with distinctive emphases regarding what it means to be a Sikh. One group, the Akhand Kirtani Jatha, draws inspiration from Bhai Randhir Singh (1878–1961), an ardent campaigner for India's freedom from British rule, who spent the years 1916 to 1930 in prison. He is one of the small, but growing number of Sikhs to have published an autobiography. This describes his unshakable adherence to his understanding of Khalsa discipline, including his insistence on eating only what had been cooked in an iron utensil – in keeping with Guru Gobind Singh's emphasis on iron/steel. (Guru Gobind Singh had described God as *sarb loh* – all iron.) Women members of the Akhand Kirtani Jatha are especially conspicuous as they wear a small under-turban beneath their *chunni* (scarf). The reason for this is that, as noted in Chapter 4, the Jatha lists among the Five Ks not *kesh* (hair) but *keski* (the headcovering in question). Their argument is that the Ks are all required of women as well as men, and that a part of the body itself cannot be one of the Five Ks. The Akhand Kirtani Jatha encourages complete equality for women in all aspects of Sikh life.

Like Bhai Randhir Singh, the Akhand Kirtani Jatha observes Khalsa discipline strictly, and requires all members to be rigorously vegetarian, to use only iron utensils in the preparation and eating of food and only to eat food prepared by members of the Jatha. The name 'Akhand Kirtani Jatha' (literally, continuous *kirtan* squad) refers to another distinctive practice, the *rain sabai* (all-night) *kirtan*. Jatha members travel far and wide to participate in these nights of continuous singing of the Gurus' hymns. Adherents' way of practising *nam simaran* entails daily recitation of the name 'Vahiguru' for an hour.

What could be called 'Nanaksar Sikhs' also incorporate into their practice the emphases of their leaders. Although followers, worshipping in gurdwaras as scattered as Smethwick, UK, and Richmond, Ontario, are now divided over who the true living Nanaksar Babaji is, all respect the holiness of Baba Nand Singh (c.1871/72–1943), a near contemporary of Bhai Randhir Singh. Baba Nand Singh showed his devotion and humility to the Gurus by his ascetic lifestyle. In Kaleran, a place in Punjab that is now marked by a magnificent white marble gurdwara, he meditated below ground level, and he described how Guru Nanak appeared before him, from out of the Guru Granth Sahib.

Many Sikhs are unaware of the dedication of the Tat Khalsa and the Akalis to establishing a strong, purified Sikhism, and know little of the competing reform movements. But they are acutely aware of different degrees of commitment to Sikhi. In conversation 'proper Sikhs' emerge as a sub-group of 'Sikhs'. 'Proper Sikhs' are *amritdhari* (initiated members of the Khalsa) or at the very least *keshdhari* (a term for those whose hair, including of course moustache and beard, has not been cut or shaved). Sikhs, more generally, include people referred to more technically as *sahajdhari* and *patit*. *Sahajdhari* is explained as 'slow adopter', a term applied to anyone who identifies as Sikh but who is not *keshdhari* and does not observe the Khalsa discipline. *Patit* (literally, 'lapsed'), denotes a Khalsa Sikh who has failed to observe some or all of the codes of discipline.

None of these terms is a good fit for the many Sikhs who have cut their hair and the growing number of individuals who identify themselves unwaveringly as Sikh, but who have no intention of ultimately observing Khalsa discipline. Many such Sikhs live outside India, and overseas Sikhs are the focus of Chapter 6.

Chapter 6
Sikhism outside India

Diaspora, the Greek word for the Jewish dispersal, is now widely used for faith communities resident in countries other than their historical homeland, whether or not their emigration and settlement resulted from traumatic events. The more than one million Sikhs resident outside India add up to at least 5% of the global Sikh population. This is a much smaller percentage than the Jewish diaspora in relation to the State of Israel. Nevertheless, in relation to co-religionists in India, the Sikh diaspora is a far higher percentage than the comparable number of diaspora Hindus in relation to the 800 million or so Hindus in India. Moreover, the greater affluence of overseas Sikh communities, especially in the UK and North America, has increased their relative importance. Account must be taken of the Sikh diaspora in any discussion of the 21st-century Panth.

This chapter reports ways in which changed circumstances have affected Sikh practice (for example, getting married only at weekends) and ways in which Sikhs have impacted on the societies in which they live (becoming integrated in a wider and wider range of occupations and activities whilst also gaining a higher public profile and enhancing the skyline with increasingly impressive gurdwaras). For over a century, Sikhs have struggled to maintain the Khalsa form in the face of social and legal constraints. What follows shows too the interaction between political and religious currents in Punjab and developments in far-flung Sikh communities.

Use of the term 'Sikh diaspora' should not be allowed to obscure the fact that migration was not specific to a single sharply defined faith community. Particularly in the case of the lowest caste groups, the Sikh–Hindu divide has sometimes been ambiguous and shifting. Nor were the causes of migration in the main faith-related: Punjabi Hindus and (in their smaller numbers) Christians, were economic migrants to the UK from the 1950s onwards along with their Sikh fellow-Punjabis. It is true that the peasant land-owners of the Jalandhar Doaba, the tongue of land drained by the Satluj and Beas rivers, were particularly motivated to migrate by the dwindling size of their holdings, as fathers successively divided holdings between their sons, and that these men were Jat by caste and Sikh by religious affiliation. But Sikh, Hindu, and Christian were driven by common concern to better their families' fortunes, and thus their *izzat*, in particular by earning money for their sisters' marriage settlements. 'Push' factors of this sort dovetailed with 'pull' factors in the overseas destinations concerned: 1950s Britain, for example, was short of labour in low-paid jobs in factories, foundries, and public transport.

Phases of migration

Whereas Indians from some other parts of India had moved overseas earlier – to the plantations of Fiji, for example, in the late 19th century – Sikhs have lived outside South Asia, at least in sizeable concentrations, only since the last decade of the 19th century. However, as the *janam-sakhi* accounts of Guru Nanak's travels as far as Sri Lanka and Mecca suggest, some Punjabis may have been travelling centuries earlier. The British annexation of Punjab in 1849 resulted in unprecedented mobilization. Sikh farmers from the east of the state were encouraged to move to the 'canal colonies' in newly irrigated areas of West Punjab (the area of Punjab that is now in Pakistan). Sikh men were recruited for the army in disproportionately higher numbers than were recruited from other communities in India.

Migration outside Punjab, and beyond India, usually by ex-servicemen, quickly followed. One hundred Sikh police arrived in Hong Kong in 1867, and until 1952 many Sikhs served in the island's police force. From here some Sikhs moved to Australia and New Zealand in the 1890s. Through army connections, some Sikhs had also migrated to Malaya, although the first Sikhs in Singapore (at that time a penal colony in Malaya) arrived in the 1850s as political prisoners after the second Sikh war. By 1921, there were more than 8,000 Sikhs in Malaya. From there some had earlier set out for new lives in Australia and New Zealand, although the first Sikhs to reach Australia had come direct from India as camel-drivers to central Australia in 1860. Some Sikhs migrated from Malaya to Thailand – many are Namdharis from West Punjab.

Sikh settlement in what later became Tanzania, Kenya, and Uganda, began – as it did for the many 'East African Asians' from Gujarat, further south than Punjab – with the British administration's need in the 1890s for men with construction skills. In 1892, Kenya's first gurdwara was opened. Between 1897 and 1901, thousands of Punjabis (in fact mostly Muslims) were recruited as indentured labourers to build the Uganda railway. The Sikh recruits were skilled artisans from the woodworking, blacksmith, and mason castes. Collectively, they came to refer to themselves by the more distinguished title of Ramgarhia. (A famous *misal* leader from the carpenter caste had assumed this title during the warfare of the 18th century.) Although the initial indentured labourers returned to Punjab, other Sikhs came out to serve in the East African Rifles. Sikhs also migrated to East Africa as skilled workers, and established themselves as a successful middle tier in colonial society, many in professional positions.

A glimpse of one Sikh's experience of childhood in Kenya comes from the reminiscences, in his book *Interculturalism, Education and Inclusion* (2000), of Jagdish Gundara, a professor in the University of London:

My home was Kenya ... My father, a Sikh, was a forester at
Ngong ... The concept of a proud but independent, egalitarian Sikh
nurtured through the stories of the Gurus, told passionately by
my mother, thrived only in the dark of my imagination ....

Over 50% of Sikhs outside India now live in North America. A Sikh
regiment visited British Columbia in 1887 en route from Queen
Victoria's Jubilee in London to India. It is unclear whether this visit
was connected with the subsequent arrival of Sikhs from South
East Asia, and the employment of many Sikhs in the lumber
industry. Between 1903 and 1908, the number of Sikhs in British
Columbia increased from 300 to 5,000. Further south, the first
four Sikhs reached California in 1899, to be followed by many who
settled and, as they were not permitted to bring in wives from the
Punjab or to marry white women, in time many married Mexicans
and brought up their children as Spanish-speaking Catholics. The
first decades of the 20th century were marked by hostility to the
'Hindus'. In 1907, for example, an Anti-Hindu Riot erupted in
Washington. Legislation soon restricted immigration to the United
States and Canada. But by the 1960s, both countries had opened up
to migration from India, and the 1970s and 1980s saw a major
influx of Sikhs, as well as other Indians. In 2000, Ujjal Singh
Dosanjh was elected premier of the Canadian province of British
Columbia.

The United Kingdom

Britain's Sikh diaspora story begins with princes and pedlars, rather
than soldiers. The exiled Duleep Singh, Maharaja Ranjit Singh's
son, who had been deposed by the British East India Company after
the Anglo-Sikh wars, arrived in Britain at the age of 15 in 1854. He
lived much of his life as 'Queen Victoria's Maharajah', and as squire
of the Suffolk village of Elveden. Another early sojourner, and
probably the first Ramgarhia Sikh in Britain, was Ram Singh. As a
talented student of Lockwood Kipling (the writer Rudyard Kipling's
father) in the Lahore School of Art, he came with him in 1891 to

create the Durbar Room of Osborne House, Queen Victoria's palatial residence on the Isle of Wight.

A few years later, Sikh students persuaded the visiting Maharaja Bhupinder Singh of Patiala to make a donation for the UK's first gurdwara, which opened in 1911 in Putney, London.

But from the First World War until the 1950s the vast majority of Sikh settlers in Britain were from a much less privileged background. In India Bhatras (as their caste was known) were perceived by others as low-status, itinerant fortune-tellers. Many UK Bhatras' families originated from the Sialkot area (now in Pakistan). Pioneering Bhatra Sikhs settled in London, in the seaports of Bristol, Cardiff, Glasgow, Portsmouth, Southampton, and Swansea, and inland in Birmingham, Edinburgh, Manchester, and Nottingham. From working as door-to-door salesmen Bhatra men moved into shopkeeping, letting property, and, of more recent generations, into a wide range of occupations and professions. Bhatras preserved customs that had been abandoned by other Sikhs, or which were unfamiliar to them. In the gurdwaras wives are totally veiled because of the presence of their senior male in-laws, and many young women have been discouraged from working outside the home. Education, especially for girls, was not so highly valued as in other Sikh caste-communities, and marriages have tended to take place at an early age. By the end of the 20th century, moves were afoot to replace the stigmatized name 'Bhatra' with the title 'Bhat'.

Next to arrive in Britain in significant numbers were Sikh men from the Jat caste, the peasant, land-owning class of rural Punjab. Individual holdings had dwindled as they were divided between sons in successive generations, but *izzat* had to be maintained, and this necessitated giving impressive dowries as well as constructing smart houses. Between 1959 and 1963 particularly, because of British immigration policy and the availability of work vouchers, young Jat men found emigration to Britain an appealing prospect.

Most cut their hair and removed their turbans, in a bid to be more employable. Wives joined them later and, unlike the Bhatra women, entered the workforce.

The third substantial Sikh migration to the UK, around 1970, was not from Punjab but from the newly independent countries of East Africa. With the rise of the dictator Idi Amin in Uganda and the Africanization policy in other East African states, many Ramgarhia Sikhs arrived in Britain, together with other 'Asians' (mainly of Gujarati, rather than Punjabi, background). The Ramgarhias joined family members who had migrated direct from India. Accustomed to maintaining a distinct identity overseas, they saw less reason to cut their hair than the Jats had. In East Africa Ramgarhia men had tended to wear only white turbans, and these still predominate in Ramgarhia congregations in the UK.

In the 1950s and 1960s, another caste-specific community had settled in Southall, Coventry, Birmingham, and Wolverhampton. Chamar by caste (and so associated by higher-caste Punjabis with skinning and tanning), many identified themselves as primarily Ravidasis, rather than as Hindus or Sikhs. As Ravidasis they took their name from the *bhagat* Ravidas. Although, unlike higher-caste Sikhs, they venerated Ravidas as Guru, in most respects their way of worship in Ravidasi gurdwaras, with the Guru Granth Sahib on its *palki*, was Sikh rather than Hindu.

By the end of the 20th century many British Sikhs had migrated to North America and Afghan Sikhs had arrived in the UK and Germany, seeking asylum from Afghanistan's Taliban regime in the 1990s.

Gurdwaras

Far from their homeland, Sikhs (including many who were not 'religious' before migration) found solace in gathering together for *kirtan* and *langar*, and bonding with others in a culturally familiar

17. **Hard-won public recognition of Sikh diaspora communities is symbolized here by the first visit of Queen Elizabeth II and Prince Philip to a gurdwara, the Sri Guru Singh Sabha Gurdwara in Hounslow, London, in October 2004**

ambience. The Guru Granth Sahib was brought to Vancouver in 1904 and the first gurdwara opened in 1908. In the USA by 1915 a gurdwara had been established in Stockton, California. Influenced by surrounding social norms, members of the *sangat* could sit on chairs in the presence of the Guru Granth Sahib, until a later generation of incoming Sikhs restored the more respectful Punjabi practice of sitting on the floor. In diaspora gurdwaras the use of chairs and tables in the *langar* was widespread until the 1990s. Other effects of living in North America on Sikhs in the first half of the 20th century are recounted by a Canadian Sikh, Tara Singh Bains:

> The ones who stayed started to cut their hair and shave, and gradually their numbers superseded the bearded Sikhs. Those clean-shaven Sikhs wanted to attend congregation in the gurdwara without wearing turbans ... They made an arrangement of nice wooden pegs for hanging hats inside the veranda at the entrance. This was at most gurdwaras.

In the UK most *sangat*s would gather in a house in which the Guru Granth Sahib had been installed until, in the 1960s and 1970s, funds were raised for the purchase of properties (including disused churches) for conversion into gurdwaras. The increasingly numerous purpose-built premises went through successive transformations into, in some cases, impressively vast, domed buildings, lined with marble. Their architects' inspiration came from the gurdwaras on historic sites in Punjab. Over time imaginative innovations included the stained glass windows in Sri Guru Singh Sabha, Southall, and the lowered floor in part of its main hall which allows worshippers in wheelchairs to enter the presence of the Guru Granth Sahib. (The requirement that everyone sit on the floor and so at a lower level than the scriptures had previously debarred them.)

Most diaspora gurdwaras are managed by an elected committee, with competition for such offices as president, secretary and treasurer. But an increasing number of gurdwaras have been set up through the dedication of a *sangat* to a charismatic personality, a Sant or *baba*. A Sant's followers express relief that their gurdwara has escaped the tensions generated by elections and his appointees are happy to perform *seva* in their designated capacity.

Whatever the style of management, gurdwaras serve overseas Sikhs as *de facto* community centres, and as a social hub for the elderly. Marriages too take place in gurdwaras every weekend, whereas in India the bride's family pick another venue. Many diaspora gurdwaras have a small library and rooms are available for children's classes.

Non-Sikhs are welcome, and need to observe the following norms:

i) Wear clothing in which you can comfortably and decently sit cross-legged.

ii) Cover your head with a scarf (females) or a white handkerchief (males) or with one of the head-coverings usually provided near the entrance.

iii) Remove footwear on entering the building and place in the shoe-rack.

iv) On entering the main hall, pay your respects to the Guru Granth Sahib (the convention is to kneel and touch the floor with your forehead).

v) When sitting, avoid pointing your feet towards the scriptures.

vi) If offered *karah prashad*, receive it reverently in your cupped hands, and eat it by picking it up with your right hand from your left palm.

vii) In the *langar* accept only what you will be able to eat, and eat using your right hand. (The emphasis on the right hand is not specifically Sikh, but part of general South Asian custom.)

Religious nurture

Home life, visitors, and videos from Punjab, going to the gurdwara, attending family weddings – these are some of the ways in which diaspora Sikh children absorb Sikhi. Additionally, Sikh organizations provide more formal nurturing, usually by setting up classes in gurdwaras. Many young Sikhs at some point attend classes in elementary Punjabi. A smaller number participate in *kirtan* classes, where they learn to play the tabla, the *baja* (harmonium), and to sing *shabad*s. Training in *gatka* (swordsmanship), a martial art, has become popular.

Annual Gurmat camps are set up by local and national organizations. For several days young Sikhs, whether in Singapore or Southall, follow a programme of listening to lectures on aspects of Sikhi, improving their Punjabi language skills, learning to perform *kirtan* and to attend to the scriptures by waving the *chauri*. There are turban-tying competitions, *gatka*, and sports. The camps give young Sikhs a brief immersion in gurdwara routine and a heightened sense of Sikh identity. They are also an opportunity, approved by older members of the family, for young people to meet each other. The camps provide a very different environment from schools, in which Sikh students are usually only a small minority.

In 1998, however, in Yuba City, California, the Guru Ram Das Khalsa preschool for 3 to 5 year olds opened. In 1999, the Guru Nanak School in the London Borough of Hillingdon made educational history in the UK by becoming the first Sikh voluntary-aided school, in other words, a publicly funded school allowed by law to have a specifically Sikh character.

Identity, turbans, and *kirpan*s

The circumstances of Sikhs resident outside India have made it hard to preserve a Khalsa identity. Turban-wearing Sikhs have faced challenges in addition to the experiences of racism that are common to other South Asians. The turban and, on occasion, the *kirpan* have hit the headlines in a long series of struggles (with varied outcomes) between Sikhs and various institutions.

In 1986, the US army ended religious exemptions to uniform standards. The armed forces continue to expect a clean-shaven appearance as a matter of unity and practicality, one argument being that, in the event of chemical warfare, a gas mask that leaked because of the wearer's beard could prove deadly. Additionally, the boot camp head-shaving ritual is supposed to help replace individual identity with the sort of group identity demanded by battle. In Canada in 1994, after a five-year struggle, involving the Human Rights Commission, the federal court upheld a 1990 amendment to the regulations of its Royal Mounted Police which allowed Sikh mounties to wear turbans.

In the UK in the 1960s Sikh bus drivers first in Manchester and, later, in Wolverhampton were denied the right to work wearing a turban. In both cases, the ban was eventually reversed – in Wolverhampton after a bitter struggle including one Sikh's threat to immolate himself. Throughout the rest of the 20th century, 'turban cases' continued spasmodically to erupt: in the UK in 1976 the Motor-Cycle Crash-Helmets (Religious Exemption) Act allowed Sikhs to wear turbans rather than motor-cycle crash helmets. Britain's membership of the European Union posed further challenges to the turban. The 1992 Personal Protective Equipment at Work regulations led to the 1993 European Community Directive that Sikhs must wear safety helmets, not turbans, in warehouses, but they were allowed to wear turbans on building sites.

Disputes continue to erupt over Sikhs' rights to wear the *kirpan*, in law courts in North America, for example, and compromises have been reached regarding air travel, as security considerations mean that Sikh passengers are not permitted to wear their *kirpan*s.

In both North America and Europe, schools have been the sites for sporadic controversy. In 1983, a Sikh solicitor, Sewa Singh Mandla, appealed to the House of Lords against a headmaster's refusal to allow his son Gurinder to wear a turban to his independent school. This, he contended, was an infringement of the Race Relations Act 1976. (Lord Denning, in the Court of Appeal had ruled in the headmaster's favour that Sikhs were not a 'racial group'.) Mandla's contention was that 'ethnic' embraced more than a merely racial concept and meant a cultural, linguistic, or religious community. In allowing the appeal, Lord Templeman famously pronounced the Sikhs to be 'more than a religious sect, they are almost a race and almost a nation'. In 2004, France's 6,000–7,000 Sikhs were caught up in legislation banning the wearing of religious symbols and clothing in school, a law principally intended to outlaw Muslim girls' headscarves.

In North America and the UK, the right of the very small proportion of *amritdhari* Sikh pupils to wear a *kirpan* led to careful, low-profile negotiated agreements and to highly publicized litigation. In 1994, one dispute ended with the Republican governor of California outlawing the wearing of *kirpan*s in school unless they were made incapable of use as a weapon.

The structures and pressures of living as a minority in non-Indian societies have resulted in some adaptation: for example, the registration of civil marriages in the gurdwara (as happens in the UK), the gathering of the largest congregation in gurdwaras on Sunday mornings rather than, as happens in rural Punjab, on the *sangrand* (the start of the new zodiac sign) or on the actual day of a festival. Another adaptation is the custom in Western countries of celebrating marriages at the weekend. All these are pragmatic responses to the fact that, in societies honed by Christian observance of Sunday as the Sabbath, the weekend is a time when most people are not at work.

WE ARE WITH YOU
"TO FIGHT FOR
YOUR RIGHT TO
WEAR TURBANS"

SIKHS IN HOLLAND

18. In Europe and North America, Sikhs have repeatedly campaigned against bans on wearing the turban. Sikhs from across Europe marched in Paris in January 2004 against the French government's prohibition of 'religious symbols' in state schools

Religious education in the UK

In the UK schools play a distinctive role in the public perception of Sikhs, and in the understanding of what being a Sikh means. In contrast to the situation in most countries, religious education, as a non-confessional subject in the curriculum, is statutory. In 1988, the Education Reform Act spelled out that in the primary and secondary schools of England and Wales religious education syllabuses must take account not only of Christianity but also of the 'teaching and practices of the other principal religions represented in Britain'. Religious educationists understood these to include Sikhism, and the development of courses and materials which had been underway since the early 1970s, particularly in cities with Sikh populations, received a boost from the legislation. Publications on Sikhism, many initially by Owen Cole and his co-author Piara Singh Sambhi, provided resource material. By and large, curriculum materials have presented Sikhism in a straightforwardly Khalsa mould.

Punjab politics

In the diaspora many Sikhs have participated in organizations supporting political parties in Punjab. Punjabi politics, and factionalism based on personalities as well as village and caste loyalties, have dominated gurdwara committee elections. By the 1980s, an increasingly burning and divisive question was whether Sikhs should fight for a homeland independent from India.

The activities of the London-based champion of Sikh separatism, Dr Jagjit Singh Chohan, initially won little support from Sikhs, even when in 1977 he proposed the renaming of Punjab as a Sikh homeland. He and Ganga Singh Dhillon, an American Sikh, publicly argued that Sikhs were a nation. It was outrage at Operation Bluestar that bonded Sikhs in a new unity, as many males asserted their identity by growing their hair and beards, and donning the turban. Funds flowed from overseas gurdwaras to Punjab. New organizations formed and these mobilized diaspora Sikhs: the International Sikh Youth Federation, Babbar Khalsa, and the Council of Khalistan, plus (in Canada and the USA) the World Sikh Organization. However, dissenting voices were also raised, and many Sikhs were silently not in favour of separatism. Political sentiment to a great extent corresponded to caste, with pro-Khalistan feeling strongest among the Jats, while the Ramgarhias and others remained distanced. Many gurdwaras were platforms for rallying calls to the Khalistani cause, but other gurdwaras allowed no political propaganda. This was particularly true of the 'Sant' gurdwaras.

Sants

Sants exert at least as strong a pull among the diaspora as they do in Punjab. The presence of an inspirational figure, of acclaimed sanctity, draws worshippers to the gurdwara. His exhortations to take initiation are a powerful antidote to losing touch with Sikhi, or to getting absorbed in non-religious pursuits or looking for spiritual refreshment outside the Panth. It is not long before followers are implying that the Sant is indeed the Guru manifest among them.

Here lies the nub of tensions within the Panth: orthodoxy, in its Tat Khalsa mould, is emphatic that, after Guru Gobind Singh, there can be no human Guru. From this perspective, the honour which many Sikhs accord to Sants oversteps the line. They are elevating someone to the position of Guru, but without admitting openly to this in the manner of the Namdharis and Nirankaris. Yet, some of the diaspora's most striking initiatives owe their inspiration to a Sant. The Sant is a transnational link between *sangat*s, strengthens individuals' commitment to Sikhi, and in some cases emphasizes details that are distinctive of particular spiritual predecessors in the Punjab. One example is Ajit Singh, a Sant based in the UK Midlands. He continues in the tradition of the legendary exorcist Vadbhag Singh, a relative of the later Gurus. Distinctive features of Ajit Singh's *sangat* practice include intense veneration for the *nishan sahib*, especially evident when the flagpole is clad in new cloth at the Vaisakhi festival.

Nishkam Sevak Jatha

In the UK in 1983, police estimated that 10,000 mourners attended the funeral of Sant Puran Singh. Known affectionately as Kerichowale Baba (from Kericho, his hometown in Kenyan tea-growing country), he preached the need to return to earlier Sikh practice. He inspired numerous Sikhs in the UK to take their faith seriously, to practise *nam simaran* daily, to regrow their hair, and to give up alcohol and meat. Sant Puran Singh founded the Nishkam Sevak Jatha in Birmingham. Roughly translated, the organization's title means the 'Selfless Service Squad', and the Jatha supported the campaign of protest against Lord Denning's ruling in the Mandla turban case. Under the subsequent leadership of Bhai Mohinder Singh, the Jatha has contributed energetically at local, national, and international levels. Its *seva* has included involvement in inter-faith and higher education initiatives, as well as the regilding of Harmandir Sahib and restoration of buildings at Anandpur Sahib and Nander. In 2004, Bhai Mohinder Singh was one of five Sikh *sant*s who started the *kar seva* (the cooperative cleaning of the pool surrounding Harmandir Sahib in Amritsar) and the Jatha provided daily *langar* for several thousand participants in the World Parliament of Religions in Barcelona, Spain, in 2004.

3HO

The mission of a Sant is to intensify Sikhs' devotion and to restore Panthic discipline and, in common with other spiritual paths that began in India, the Sikh faith does not seek to convert members of other communities. However, unusually, one United States-based Sant has attracted several thousand Western followers. Harbhajan Singh Puri (1929–2004) is better known as Yogi Bhajan, and his organization, Sikh Dharma of the Western Hemisphere, which he founded in California in about 1970, is better known as 3HO, the Healthy, Happy, Holy Organization. Both male and female followers dress in white, including equally tall white turbans for both, and all members take Sikh names, with the surname 'Khalsa'. As well as adhering to the *rahit*, their discipline includes meditation and kundalini yoga (a practice not generally regarded as part of Sikh tradition). Their aim is to cleanse the whole person, including the subconscious mind, of impurities in readiness for entry into the Aquarian Age.

The Sikh diaspora has allowed for the development of groupings diversified by caste and by charismatic leadership, and it has been a powerful support base for political factions in Punjab. Forms of Sikhi that affirm the Nirmala, Sevapanthi, Udasi, and Nihang emphases within the Panth, rather than the Tat Khalsa pattern, show signs of developing. (The Nirmala tradition is one of erudition and asceticism, and Sevapanthis stand for dedicated service to others.) In economic terms, diaspora Sikhs' remittances to Punjab have resulted in not only desirable residences and mechanized farming, but the rebuilding of gurdwaras on an increasingly impressive scale, and the preservation of Sikhs' religious and historical heritage, in, for example, the Smithsonian Sikh Gallery in Washington. Two further contributions by Sikhs overseas to the Panth are a new calendar (see Chapter 8) and fresh energy in Sikh studies.

Sikh studies

In the 1990s, Sikh scholars, mainly in North America, brought new insights into, for example, the compilation of scripture. Additionally, the sustained, destructive resistance by some conservative Sikhs in North America and in Punjab to critically open-minded, 'Western' styles of investigation is itself an aspect of late 20th-century Sikh history. What is more, in the diaspora Sikh studies (like the inclusion of Sikhism in British schools' religious education curriculum) recurrently interacts with Sikhs' projection of a distinct identity. Increasingly, too, litigation in turban and sword disputes has required scholars in Sikh studies to provide authoritative statements. For example, Hew McLeod served as an 'expert witness' in the Canadian court case which ended in the vindication of Sikh mounties' right to wear the turban.

Sikh studies has developed as an interdisciplinary area, within the broader field of South Asian studies, and involved non-Sikh as well as Sikh scholars. It was McLeod's rigorous application of textual analysis and source criticism to the *janam-sakhi* literature which took the study of Guru Nanak beyond hagiography and confessional reiteration of tradition. Over more than three decades, his publications raised and addressed issues in every century of Sikh history. These included the question of Sikh identity in relation to caste and to the Khalsa *rahit-nama*s.

In North America, Sikh studies conferences were successfully held in Berkeley in 1979 and Toronto in 1987, and financial backing was forthcoming from *sangat*s and individual patrons, notably the fibre optics magnate Narinder Singh Kapany. Initiatives in Sikh studies in the universities of Toronto, British Columbia, Columbia (New York), Michigan, and Santa Barbara (California) have contributed robustly to Sikh studies.

Sadly, McLeod became *persona non grata* to conservative Sikhs, particularly at the Institute of Sikh Studies in Chandigarh, Punjab, and its allies in North America. In turn, his former students, Pashaura Singh and Harjot Oberoi (who had been appointed to a Chair in British Columbia), were denounced by hostile Sikhs. Pashaura Singh's thesis on the Adi Granth had been photocopied without authorization, copies were circulated and articles accusing him of blasphemy followed; he was required to do penance by the SGPC in Amritsar. Sikh scholars were accused of supposed links with Christian missions, and of being tainted by Hindu aspirations to hegemony in India and a modernist, anti-traditional agenda. Resentment against individual scholars and the 'Western', or 'McLeodian', academic enterprise peaks at times of acute sensitivity to the minority status in India. Thus, in the 1980s and 1990s the unreadiness of some vocal Sikhs to accept that a fellow Sikh could write as a historian rather than confessionally coincided with the community's tension with the Indian government and the consequent feeling that as a minority Sikhs were under threat. Setbacks to funding, and so to scholarship, have resulted.

In the balanced view of Punjab's distinguished Sikh historian Jagtar Singh Grewal: 'Textual criticism is not likely to affect the Sikh doctrines' and 'the Sikhs have nothing to fear from genuine textual criticism'. Despite their vulnerability to Sikh attacks and the removal of their academic posts, diaspora Sikh scholars, in active dialogue with non-Sikh colleagues in the field, opened up Sikh studies to debate and development in a way that Sikh scholars in Punjab could not have done at that time. Sikh studies became increasingly interdisciplinary, moving from the dominance of history to areas such as philosophy, comparative literature, and gender studies. Key areas of lively debate include the text of the Adi Granth and the Dasam Granth, the origins of the Five Ks, the role of the Singh Sabha in defining the Panth, the phenomenon of martyrdom, as well as the development of the diaspora. They also include the social dynamics of caste and gender, the remit of Chapter 7.

Chapter 7
Attitudes to caste, gender, and other faiths

Sundri and Jess

Two works of fiction frame the 20th century, one a historical novel, the other a film. *Sundri*, the first novel in Punjabi, was published in 1898 by a man, the Singh Sabha intellectual Bhai Vir Singh. His heroine, Sundri, an imaginary 18th-century Sikh woman, was a paragon of saintly womanhood, whose selfless courage culminated in martyrdom for her faith. Bhai Vir Singh drew overt comparisons between her courageous devotion and her Hindu and Muslim counterparts' moral deficiency, and the defiance which Sundri and her Khalsa brother showed towards her Muslim abductor contrasts with their Hindu parents' submissiveness.

Bend It Like Beckham, released in 2002, was the first English film to focus on a Sikh woman. The film's director, Gurinder Chadha, and Parminder Nagra, the actress who plays the leading part, are both Sikh women: the film is a celebration of creative female agency. Jesminder Bhamra, or 'Jess', the principal character, is a British-born and football-mad young woman. Jess shows her skills not only on the football pitch but also in negotiating relationships within her family, which (like Gurinder Chadha's) is a Ramgarhia Sikh family from East Africa. In the film the differences between 'Asian' and 'English' individuals' assumptions about relationships point up hiatuses between cultures and generations, but these are not presented in terms of religious difference. Gaps there are, but the boundaries are to be spanned, furtively or exuberantly.

Jess's religious faith is not to the fore, yet her struggle to compete in a man's sporting world echoes a motif in the Sikh tradition, exemplified by Mai Bhago, an 18th-century Sikh woman who moved into battle ahead of the men.

This chapter picks up the theme of gender, as well as caste and other faiths, in relation to earlier chapters' discussions of Punjabi cultural norms, the Gurus' insights, and the legacy of Guru Gobind Singh both in the Khalsa and in the Dasam Granth. Also centre stage are the strictures of successive *rahit-nama*s and the reformist project of the Singh Sabha, plus more recent developments, especially in the diaspora. These sets of issues belong together in any discussion of Sikhs' resounding claims that the Panth is egalitarian, or at least that the Gurus taught that *mukti* (liberation from rebirth) is open to all alike.

A verse of Guru Nanak's provides the religious benchmark:

> Call everyone noble, none is lowborn: there is only one potter, God, who has fashioned everyone alike. God's is the one light that pervades all creation.
>
> (AG 62)

Here, certainly, is encouragement to respect everyone regardless of their sex, caste, or religious label.

Gender

The American Sikh scholar Nikky-Guninder Kaur Singh has argued that the very fact that in Punjabi the noun *bani*, for the utterance of the Gurus, is feminine valorizes the feminine principle. What is more certain is that Professor Nikky Singh broke important ground by offering a feminist interpretation of Sikh tradition.

Consistently with the majority of the world's scriptures, no women contributed to the Guru Granth Sahib. It is true that a verse by Mira Bai, a celebrated woman devotee of Krishna, is preserved in the Banno *bir*, a recension of the scripture that differs in places from the accepted version, but it does not appear in the Damdami *bir*. It was probably excluded from the canon, however, not because the author was a woman, but because she expressed devotion to God in incarnate form as the attractive Lord Krishna, rather than to God as formless and beyond human attributes.

In Sikh apologetic, Guru Nanak is heralded as championing women and the following verses are often quoted:

> Our birth is from a woman and in a woman we grow. We are engaged to and wed a woman. Woman is our friend and from woman comes the family. If one woman dies we seek another; without woman there can be no bond. Why call woman bad when she gives birth to rajas? Woman herself is born of a woman, and none comes into this world without her. Nanak, only the True One alone is independent of woman.
>
> (AG 473)

The lines hail woman primarily as instrumentally necessary for the continuity of humankind, and Guru Nanak also unequivocally challenged the prevalent Hindu view of childbirth as polluting:

> If pollution attaches to birth, then pollution is everywhere.
> Cow-dung [fuel] and firewood breed maggots;
> Not one grain of corn is without life;
> Water itself is a living substance, imparting life to all vegetation.
>
> (AG 472)

Women provide challenging images throughout the text. The view in parts of Hindu society that the ideal course of action for a widow was to die on her husband's funeral pyre is the basis for one of Guru Amar Das's verses:

> They are not satis who are burnt alive on the pyres; rather satis are
> they who die of the blow of separation.

> (AG 787)

In other images women appear, as part of *maya*, to be a distraction
from *mukti*.

As earlier chapters have already mentioned, the grammatical
requirements of the English language, which cannot express much
without resorting to pronouns, together with the influence of
Christian beliefs about God, have influenced English translations of
the Guru Granth Sahib, so that the masculine is emphasized. This
has happened despite Guru Nanak's statement that:

> The wise and beauteous Being (*purakh*) is neither a man nor a
> woman nor a bird.

> (AG 1010)

and Guru Arjan's affirmation that, echoing a widely known Hindu
verse:

> You are my father, you are my mother,
> You are my kinsman, you are my brother.

> (AG 103)

Nikky Singh used the gender-neutral word 'sovereign' where earlier
translators had used 'God' and 'Lord', and today's scholars are
assiduously avoiding 'he', 'him', and 'his' in sentences about the
divine principle. However, like Vahiguru, the terms 'Akal Purakh'
and 'Karta Purakh', as well as 'Sahib', carry a masculine association
for speakers of North Indian languages. As such, they require
masculine endings for any associated verbs or adjectives. But this
grammatical fact should perhaps count for no more than *bani*'s
feminine gender.

The Sikh literature that unequivocally exalts the divine as Durga, the Goddess, is a composition, traditionally attributed to Guru Gobind Singh in the Dasam Granth. However, Sikh unease since Singh Sabha times with the unmistakably Hindu character of this celebration of the Goddess makes even the most feminist of Sikhs cautious. This is because it jeopardizes Sikh presentation of the Guru as monotheistic. Durga, if understood in any but a metaphorical way, belongs to the Hindu world view against which Sikhs have been defining themselves more and more vocally ever since the late 19th century.

Instead, Sikhs welcome unequivocally the image of the soul's relationship with the divine in terms of the (female) beloved's relationship with her bridegroom:

> The Lord is my husband, I his wife. The Lord is immensely great, I am so small.
>
> (AG 483)

The stanzas by Guru Ram Das that are central to every Anand Karaj marriage express the movement of the individual soul towards God by analogy with the bride's union with her lord. For the devout Sikh the message is clear and underlines the fact that the sex of the devotee is irrelevant to spiritual progress. At the same time, the conjugal image reinforces a subliminal acknowledgement of God as masculine, even while allowing men to affirm their own feminine aspect in their devotion.

*Rahit-nama*s include both instruction to men on their behaviour to women and statements of how women should behave. For example, according to the late 18th-century Bhai Desa Singh *rahit-nama*, men should treat all women other than their own wives as if they were their daughters or their mothers. The Chaupa Singh *rahit-nama* makes it clear that women should learn to read the Guru Granth Sahib, but not do so in public. They should not receive initiation with *amrit*, and they must be devout and modest. But the more recent Sikh Rahit Maryada adopts a different approach, making it clear that Sikhi requires obedience to the same rules by both men and women. Sikh Rahit Maryada introduces its opening definition of a Sikh with the words '*jo istari jan purush*' ('whatever woman or man') and subsequently states that women should not be veiled in the *sangat*, that they may sit in attendance on the Guru Granth Sahib, that they may be initiated and may also be members of the *panj piare* who administer initiation.

In the lives of the Gurus and subsequent Sikh history we meet not Bhai Vir Singh's heroine but another Sundri. This Sundri is one of Guru Gobind Singh's three wives. In the little that is known about her we come across what the Canadian scholar Doris Jakobsh has called the principles of both celebration and silence. Like other women who were mothers, wives, or daughters of Gurus, Sundri's role is celebrated: she is remembered for sweetening the *amrit* with which Singhs were initiated in 1699. But at the same time the record is strangely silent and uncertain. In fact, in two early records of the events of Vaisakhi 1699 the addition of sugar is attributed variously to each of the Guru's other two wives, Jito and Sahib Devi. And almost nothing is made of the fact that Sundri led the Panth for longer than any Guru after Guru Nanak.

It was Mata (Mother) Sundri who appointed Bhai Mani Singh to manage the gurdwaras in Amritsar and to compile the Dasam Granth. The record similarly tells us little about Guru Nanak's wife, Sulakhani, who is also referred to by another name, or about Bibi Bhani, the daughter of the third Guru, wife of the fourth and mother of the fifth Guru, or, for that matter, about Mata Gujari, the wife of Guru Tegh Bahadur who witnessed the brutal deaths of her grandsons.

Such contradictions are implicit in *janam-sakhi* and other narrative accounts of the Gurus' lives. Sikhi affirms family life as opposed to the Nath Yogis' insistence on celibacy, and consistently with this, Guru Nanak passed over his son Siri Chand as successor because of his Udasi (and so celibate) lifestyle. Moreover, according to Guru Nanak's *shabad*s (and the *bhagat*s' songs) salvation is open to all, regardless of gender. Yet marriage occupied apparently only a marginal place in much of Guru Nanak's life as the itinerant preacher and singer of *shabad*s.

19. During the *amrit sanskar* (initiation into the Khalsa), one of the officiating *panj piare* moistens the candidate's hair with sweetened water (the *amrit*), which had been ceremonially stirred while scriptural passages were recited

Sikhs also emphasize the Gurus' denunciation of female infanticide, a prohibition that was certainly imposed on Guru Gobind Singh's Khalsa. The social need for this ban was the prevalence of the malpractice of stifling baby girls at birth, especially in certain clans, not least the Gurus' own Bedi and Sodhi lineages.

In Sikh history, as retold by the Singh Sabha reformers and subsequent writers, individual women played a strikingly heroic role. The name of Mai Bhago is to the fore as the woman who rallied Guru Gobind Singh's forces in the battle of Muktsar in 1705, so that men whose courage had failed them died as martyrs. The Singh Sabha's interpretation of Sikh history, which forms Sikh understanding today, is that since 1699 women have (like the Sundri of Bhai Vir Singh's novel) received *amrit* on a par with men, and have as part of this initiation assumed the name 'Kaur'. This name is a form of the Hindi word *kanwar* and so is more appropriately translated as 'Prince' than its usual rendering as 'Princess'. It is possible that it only gradually came into its present widespread use as the second part of a Sikh woman's name.

Mainstream Sikh history overlooks the Namdharis' emphasis since the 19th century on male/female equality, and several other minority groups have tried to advance women's status. For instance, in the 20th century the American 3HO campaigned for women to be allowed to serve in the Golden Temple on an equal basis with men. But other minority groups are more restrictive than the majority of the Panth. Thus Chapter 6 mentioned the strictness of the Bhatra caste in the UK, and the specific requirements which Sants impose on their *sangat*s include, for example, Ajit Singh's rule that (because they may be menstruating and hence impure) women keep their distance from the *nishan sahib* during its annual ceremonial cleansing.

However, when non-Sikhs visit a gurdwara they are often favourably surprised to see a woman publicly reading from the scriptures and men distributing food in the *langar*, and they comment on the striking evidence of the equality of men and women. At the same time, in Sikh society, as in other societies, both men and women acquire and pass on a complex of spoken and unspoken norms about gender roles. Moreover, certain religious roles are almost always played by men. The *panj piare*, whether marching in festival processions or administering *amrit* in the *khande di pahul* ceremony, are nearly always male. It is true that in North America, from the 1970s, there have been instances of females taking this part among Akhand Kirtani Jatha and 3HO *sangat*s, but these are exceptions. In the 1980s, the militant Sant Jarnail Singh Bhindranwale refused to allow women to be *panj piare* because no woman had responded to Guru Gobind Singh's invitation in 1699 (an argument uncannily similar to Christian arguments against the ordination of women on the grounds that none of Jesus's twelve disciples was a woman).

Conspicuously, 3HO women wear tall white turbans of the same style as their male counterparts, and Akhand Kirtani Jatha women wear the *keski*, which is a small turban, usually of black cloth. Despite this, and the fact that contemporary Khalsa discipline, including the five Ks, is unisex, Sikhism retains the strikingly masculine image of the turbaned male *keshdhari* Sikh.

In the running of gurdwaras there remain persistent imbalances: on gurdwara committees men far outnumber women, and only one woman, Bibi Jagir Kaur, has been president of the SGPC. Sants too are almost without exception men. The occasional exception is referred to as 'Bibi' not 'Baba', for example Bibi Nihal Kaur of the Mastuana tradition in Punjab and Bibi Balwant Kaur of the Bebe Nanaki Gurdwara in Birmingham.

As we have seen, Sikh teaching emphasizes the married life over the celibate life. In the Anand marriage rite, as the couple walk slowly around the Guru Granth Sahib, what the outsider sees is the bride, in each circuit, following behind the groom. But what a devout Sikh may perceive is that both the man and the woman are at an equal

20. Many 3HO Sikh women, as well as men, wear white turbans. The Healthy, Happy, Holy Organization (Sikh Dharma of the Western Hemisphere), established in California by Harbhajan Singh Puri (Yogi Bhajan), emphasizes the equality of women in the Khalsa as well as meditation and physical fitness

distance from their Guru, and that a woman's role is equal but different. During the ceremony the groom is told to be the 'protector of the bride's person and honour', the bride is then exhorted to regard her husband as 'master of all love and respect'.

Marriage needs to be understood in terms of Punjabi society as well as religious principles and liturgy. Nowhere is the tension between Punjabi culture and Sikh insights more powerful, and nowhere is the influence of Hindu/Indic tradition more evident, than in the red and gold finery, the financial calculations and expenditure, the customary banter, and expressions of triumph on the groom's side and the grief (at the girl's departure) among the bride's family. The reformist calls of the Namdhari Gurus and others for plain white attire and modest outlay (by, for example, holding joint ceremonies for a number of couples) have not impacted on the Panth as a whole.

Discussion of the extent to which marriages are arranged (or at least approved) by senior members of the couple's families, and the increasing tendency for couples to initiate the relationship, could occupy a whole book, given the mix of conservatism and change in rural Punjab, urban India, and the diaspora. In the diaspora a small number of Sikh women run away from home to avoid the pressure of maintaining the family's *izzat* by consenting to an unwelcome match. As in South Asian families of other faith communities, the costs for parents that result from marrying their daughters in a style which will avoid loss of face are rising, whether in London, Los Angeles, or Ludhiana. Among overseas communities the incidence of divorce and remarriage is also increasing rapidly, as couples face the pressures of society at large as well as those of meeting family expectations and getting to know each other better.

Yet the fact remains that in much of Sikh society, as in South Asian society more generally, a woman's standing depends largely upon having a husband. Some Sikh women observe the Punjabi Hindu annual fast on the day of Karva Chauth for their husband's welfare. A divorced woman is referred to as discarded (*chhadi-hoi*) and the word for a widow is a term of abuse in Punjabi.

The persistently unequal number of girls and boys in Sikh society – as in Punjabi society as a whole – is related to the burden which daughters represent to many parents. In order to avoid the shame of being wife-givers rather than bride-receivers, some Khatri and Jat families for generations ensured that most surviving children were male.

Sophisticated technology provides new ways of sex selection. In the late 20th century developments in medical technology combined with families' preference for sons to precipitate the emergence of laboratories and clinics providing ultra-sonar screening of pregnant women and abortions of unwanted female foetuses. The juvenile sex ratio in Punjab, the one majority Sikh state, has declined with each successive census, and the fall in the number of female children accelerated sharply between 1991 and 2001, so that there are fewer than eight girls born for every ten boys. In order to check sex-selective foeticide, in 1996 in India the Pre-Natal Diagnostic Techniques (Regulation and Prevention of Misuse) Act 1994 came into force. Despite some crack-downs, the killing of girls before birth continues. The Punjabi concern with maintaining *izzat* clearly militates against the religious prohibition of female infanticide, as enshrined in the Sikh Rahit Maryada.

It is a moot point whether the relative affluence of relatives in the diaspora, and the impact of globalization and consumerism on Punjab, as well as on India's cities, have emancipated or oppressed women. Certainly, the unborn Punjabi female is at greater risk than ever before. At the same time, more Sikh women than ever before have significant public roles. The humanitarian service of Dr Inderjit Kaur, of the All India Pingalwara Charitable Society, provides one sterling example. Another is the original artistry of exquisite contemporary miniatures by the UK-based Sikh twin artists, Rabindra and Amrit Kaur Singh.

Caste

Not only gender but also caste affect individual Sikhs' experience. But what does 'caste' mean? And how significant is it? The (originally Portuguese) word 'caste' in English refers to two components of India's social structure, which are much discussed in literature on the Hindu tradition, under their Sanskrit names of *varna* and *jati*. *Varna* (*varan* in Punjabi) is applied to the tiers ('classes') in the fourfold hierarchy which has Brahmins (the priestly class) at the top, above Kshatriyas, Vaishyas, and (in lowest place) Shudras. *Jati* (*zat* or *zat-biradari* in modern Punjabi), on the other hand, signifies the multitude of occupational groups such as potters, goldsmiths, and tailors. All over India these occupational groups have for many centuries been endogamous – a potter's son could marry a potter's daughter but not a tailor's or a farmer's. People have looked down on some *jati*s and looked up to others according to their respective positions on the ladder of *varna*. Two *jati*s suffered more oppression than any of the others and were regarded as outside the *varna* hierarchy as their castes specialized in the unclean occupations of skinning and tanning and of sweeping, which could include the removal of excrement. Members of these two communities, the Chamars and the Chuhras respectively, increasingly prefer the designation *dalit* (literally, 'oppressed').

During the 20th century an unprecedented rate of change (including urbanization, education, and migration) unsettled the traditional relations between the many *jati*s, but assumptions and stereotypes persisted, as did caste as a criterion for selecting eligible spouses. Moreover, probably to a greater extent than elsewhere, in the UK the names 'Bhatra' and 'Ramgarhia' figure in the titles of many gurdwaras.

All this is particularly puzzling for anyone, Sikh or non-Sikh, who has learned that 'the Gurus were reformers who abolished the caste system' or that 'caste is Hindu, not Sikh'. You may have read elsewhere that Sikhism does away with *varnashrama-dharma*, the Hindu ideal of religious duties that vary according to one's stage in life and one's hereditary position. For instance, Owen Cole and Piara Singh Sambhi quote the Sikh dictum that:

> A Sikh should be a Brahmin in piety, a Kshatriya in defence of truth and the oppressed, a Vaishya in business acumen and hard work, and a Shudra in serving humanity. A Sikh should be all castes in one person, who should be above caste.

The Gurus, like the Bhagats Namdev, Kabir, and Ravidas, proclaimed the irrelevance of people's inherited status to their spiritual destiny. In Guru Nanak's view:

Worthless is caste (*jati*) and worthless an exalted name,
For all humanity there is but a single refuge.

(AG 83)

and

There is no *jati* in the hereafter.

(AG 349)

Similarly, according to Guru Amar Das:

When you die you do not carry your *jati* with you:
It is your deeds which determine your fate.

(AG 363)

So too Guru Arjan declared:

This divine teaching is for everyone, Brahmin, Kshatriya, Vaishya and Shudra.

(AG 747)

The very fact that the (higher-caste) Gurus included in the Sikh scriptures the compositions of a *bhagat*, Kabir (who was a weaver by *jati*), Namdev (a tailor), and Ravidas (from the skinning and tanning *jati*) suggests their disregard for caste as spiritually irrelevant. (The Gurus' Khatri caste is usually regarded as Kshatriya.)

Indeed, what we know about the Gurus' lives points to a strong critique of caste divisions and a public devaluing of caste in the Panth's key institutions. The *langar* subverted brahminical rules about commensality, according to which only caste fellows could eat together and higher-caste individuals could not receive food cooked by members of lower castes. Not only did Guru Gobind Singh's *panj piare* come from *jati*s of varied ranking on the scale of *varna*, and shed their caste-specific names, but the *khande di pahul* rite involved all candidates in drinking the *amrit* from the same iron bowl, and finishing the residue in reverse order. This was an unthinkable act according to the rules of purity and pollution that shored up the hierarchy of castes, since sharing a utensil which had been in contact with another person's saliva would be particularly polluting.

As we saw in Chapter 5, in their competition with the Hindu reformists' Arya Samaj, the activists of the Singh Sabha reached out to the lowest caste communities. In 1920, some new 'untouchable' converts came to the Harmandir Sahib with the intention of offering and, in their turn, receiving *karah prashad*. When higher-caste Sikhs protested, recourse was taken to the Guru Granth Sahib. The *vak* (a verse of Guru Amar Das) began as follows:

> Upon the worthless God bestows grace, if they will serve the True Guru.

> (AG 38)

The 'untouchables' had been vindicated by their Guru.

However, Punjabis of the two most disadvantaged *jatis* continue to feel more comfortable gathering in their own places of worship. Several UK cities have Ravidasi centres in addition to the gurdwaras that were established by Sikhs of higher caste. Khatri Sikhs, though not numerically strong, are respected, among them those whose surnames of Bedi and Sodhi link them to the families of Guru Nanak and the last six Gurus, respectively. Jats enjoy a long-established numerical dominance (in Punjab they make up more than 66% of the Sikh population) as well as economic clout in Punjab. At 7%, Ramgarhias are the next largest group. They honour their 18th-century forebear, Jassa Singh Ramgarhia, and some show respect, on the day after Divali, to Lord Vishvakarma, son of Brahma in the Hindu pantheon, as founder of their line as well as architect of the universe.

During the British Raj census-takers required people to record their religious allegiance and also their caste. The British administrators must take further responsibility for hardening caste divisions (as well as a rural–urban divide) as a result of the Punjab Land Alienation Act 1900 and the Punjab Pre-Emption Act 1913, as these Acts prohibited the transfer of land from land-owners to the 'non-agricultural' classes. In other words the Jats' hold on the land was secure, and their disdain for landless castes the greater.

Particularly in the diaspora, many Sikhs who, in keeping with Khalsa avoidance of caste names, used 'Singh' and 'Kaur' rather than their family name as their surname for official purposes, decided to reinstate their (often *jati*-specific) family name.

Most Sikh families continue to check out the caste of any prospective son- or daughter-in-law. Love marriages crossing caste divides often result in a parental boycott of the errant son or daughter. Fieldwork in the 1990s among young British Sikh children who had never lived in India showed the persistence of stereotypes of other castes.

Clearly, it is over-simplistic to assume that Sikhs have overturned or escaped the caste-based structure of South Asian society. But, equally, it is misleading to represent contemporary Sikhs as having in this respect somehow betrayed their Gurus. Apart from Guru Har Krishan (who died as a boy and so did not marry), all the Gurus had Khatri wives and their sons and daughters were also married within caste. Caste operates horizontally, binding together caste fellows, as well as vertically, as a segregated hierarchy. The Gurus did not condemn, or break with, the convention of marrying (and marrying their children) within the *jati*. But it is hard to reconcile the Gurus' affirmation of spiritual equality with the disowning of a child who has 'married out'. For those who obey Guru Gobind Singh's ideal for his Khalsa, the caste of individuals is irrelevant.

Other faiths

The Sikh Rahit Maryada does, however, forbid a Sikh from marrying a non-Sikh. But as with caste, it does not follow from the fact that marriage across boundaries is discouraged that members of other communities are treated disrespectfully. As we have seen with gender and caste, so too with 'other faiths', the Sikh scripture provides inspiration towards transcending barriers, even though Sikh history indicates some tensions. And inter-faith partnerships are increasing.

To return to the novel *Sundri*: Bhai Vir Singh spells out his heroine's superiority to Muslim and Hindu women. At the same time, Sundri's virtuous conduct includes nursing not only Sikhs but also Hindus, Pathans, and Mughals. Her impartial dedication to relieve suffering is reminiscent of Guru Gobind Singh's follower Bhai Kahnaiya, who gave water to the fallen warriors on both sides in battle, attracting the Guru's commendation.

In perfect unison with his predecessors, Guru Gobind Singh proclaimed in a composition entitled 'Akal Ustat':

> Hindus and Muslims are one!
> The same Lord is the creator and nourisher of all.
> Recognise no distinctions between them.
> The temple and the mosque are the same,
> So are puja and namaz.
> People are all one.

(DG 28)

Neither the Dasam Granth nor the Adi Granth leave any doubt that distinctions based on religious identification are (like those based on gender and caste) ultimately immaterial. Twenty-first century Sikhs point out with pride that the Adi Granth consists of writings by *bhagat*s from 'other faiths', with reference to the fact that Shaikh Farid was a Muslim and many contributors were Hindu. Sikhs are happy to accept the popular tradition that, at Guru Arjan's request, the Muslim saint Mian Mir laid the foundation stone of the Harmandir Sahib. Guru Tegh Bahadar's death is portrayed as martyrdom to defend the freedom of faith of those of another religion (the Kashmiri Brahmins). Maharaja Ranjit Singh's celebrated reign allowed religious freedom, with Muslims and Hindus alike in high office. Moreover, on his death, his *ranis* committed *sati* on his funeral pyre. While retrospectively hardening the boundaries between 'religions', Sikhs continually stress the respect which Sikhi instils for other faiths.

Centuries of intermittent warfare in Punjab have also left their mark on Sikh attitudes. At a time of violent hostility between Sikhs and Mughal armies, Guru Gobind Singh ordered the social segregation of his Khalsa from Muslims, and successive *rahit-namas* reiterated this. There have also been recurrent strains between the Panth and the Hindu society in which it is embedded. Two centuries after Guru Gobind Singh, Bhai Vir Singh and the Singh Sabha proclaimed the superiority of Sikhi to (Hindu) superstitions. The Tat Khalsa and the Akalis of the early 20th century worked for a firmer boundary between Sikh and Hindu tradition by purging gurdwaras of image-worship and advocating distinct life-cycle rites for the Panth. In 1947 Partition triggered an outburst of violence between Sikhs and Muslims on an unprecedented scale. The 1980s and 1990s witnessed an upsurge of anti-Hindu feeling as violence again erupted in Punjab, and among Punjabi youth in the diaspora tensions (on university campuses, for example) sometimes follow Sikh/Muslim fault lines.

Nevertheless, Sikhs' record of respect for all faiths remains strong, and the conversion of others to Sikhi is not generally on the agenda. At the same time, the syncretistic (or inclusive) tendencies of more *sanatan* Sikhs are unacceptable in terms of the Sikh Rahit Maryada. It forbids, for example, the lighting of incense sticks and the leaving of a container of water by the Guru Granth Sahib (a popular way of obtaining healing *amrit*). Consistently with these prohibitions, part of the Sikh Rahit Maryada's definition of a Sikh is one 'who does not believe in another religion'.

The inter-faith movement, however, which gained prominence in the West in the late 20th century, strikes a chord with sympathetic Sikhs, and Sikhi leaves them free from the theological constraints of their Christian and Muslim partners' more exclusivist faiths. The Gurus' condemnation of *haumai* (ego), and the emphasis on a search for truth that is deeply experienced rather than cognitive and propositional, are conducive to respect for spiritual seekers whatever the signposts on their various paths.

In terms of gender, caste, and relations with 'other faiths' (and indeed the extent to which Sikhs perceive Hindus as 'other'), differences of interpretation are evident, and it is misleading to suggest a simple dichotomy between faith and practice. Chapter 8 will continue our examination of the contemporary scene in its complex response to the Gurus' precepts and society's pressures.

Chapter 8
Sikhism and the third millennium

Religion in the 21st century

The Satanic Verses, Salman Rushdie's novel published in 1988, opens with four imaginary Sikhs hijacking a plane. Rushdie was writing at a time of escalating violence, with Kalashnikov-bearing Sikhs regarded as freedom-fighters by supporters of Khalistan and as terrorists by others. In another unfortunate elision of 'Sikh' with 'terrorist', one of the consequences of Al-Qaeda's assault on the twin towers in New York on 11 September 2001 was a series of assaults on turbaned Sikhs by other Americans, who assumed that their beards and turbans marked them out as Islamic terrorists.

Terrorism is now closely associated with religion in popular consciousness, and in particular with 'fundamentalism'. The term 'fundamentalism' was first coined with reference to early 20th-century Protestant Christians, because of their insistence upon Christian fundamentals, notably the inerrancy of the Bible as God's revealed word. By the close of the 20th century, the term 'fundamentalist' had shifted to overlap, in much of the popular media at least, with 'militant', 'extremist', and 'terrorist'. Individuals with agendas both spiritual and political rallied the faithful in resurgent (and sometimes almost unrecognizable) expressions of ancient faith traditions. In politically and economically unequal and complex situations violence all too readily took over.

This development would have astonished sociologists earlier in the 20th century who predicted the imminent demise of religion as improved material circumstances reduced the hunger for divine support, and as scientific discovery reduced faith to anachronistic superstition. In fact, an increasingly widespread disregard for religion, both privately and publicly, did and does coexist with the upsurge of religious movements and religion-related violence. Despite the apparent contradictions between these tendencies, in their strikingly varied combinations, they need and feed each other.

Sikhs, belonging as they do to their interlinked transnational communities, must be understood in this global religious context. Contemporary globalization involves the rapid movement of people and of ideas (about gender, equality, bio-ethics) and the growing importance of virtual, web-based communities. Globalization also entails the commodification of religions as optional packages of belief and practice.

By the end of the 20th century, the rapidly modernizing Punjab was the site of material consumerism of the sort that Europe and North America had experienced for several decades. Earlier in the 20th century, Khushwant Singh, a Sikh historian and journalist, had, like the Tat Khalsa reformers, voiced fears about the disappearance of Sikhism into Hinduism if too many Sikhs abandoned the Khalsa identity. But, by the end of the century, religious apathy and compulsive consumerism, rather than pervasive 'Hinduism', looked set to erode Sikhi, as many young men in Punjab opted for a more Western look. Yet, at the same time, the alacrity of young diaspora Sikhs in identifying themselves as 'Sikh', as well as 'Canadian', 'Malaysian', or whatever, regardless of their degree of religiosity, continues undiminished.

Against this backdrop, this chapter returns to the issue of Sikhism's emergence as a separate religion. Before doing so, however, it looks at the question: within the Panth where does authority lie? The discussion of caste and gender raised the question of where Sikhs are, or should be, turning for authoritative guidance on social and ethical matters. It also upset assumptions that Sikhism and Hinduism, or at least Sikh society and Indic society, were distinct from each other. The continuing relevance of these two questions is obvious in the arguments and events surrounding the implementation of the Nanakshahi calendar.

The calendar controversy

Sikhs' religious calendar consists of annual *gurpurab*s (anniversaries of the Gurus) and *mela*s (other festival celebrations). Until 2003 this calendar was based on the Hindus' Vikrami (in Punjabi, Bikrami) calendar. Like the internationally implemented Common Era (Gregorian) calendar, this follows a framework of 12 lunar months and a 365-day solar year. What differs is the means of preventing slippage between the solar cycle and the twelve lunar months. The Gregorian calendar's months are (with the exception of February in non-leap years) longer than a lunar month and, additionally, an extra day is inserted every four years. The solution of the Vikrami calendar (like the Jewish calendar) is to maintain the 28-day month and intercalate not a day but a whole month every few years, so making sure that a seasonal festival always falls in the appropriate season. Despite this correction, one result is that (as Hindus and Jews know all too well) each religious anniversary falls on a different Gregorian date each year. More worryingly for Sikhs, in some years Guru Gobind Singh's birthday would appear twice, at the beginning of January and at the end of December. The date of Vaisakhi (a solar rather than a lunar date) was also set to shift from spring to autumn over the next ten millennia, as the Vikrami solar year differs from the more precisely calibrated Gregorian year by some 20 minutes. A Canadian Sikh,

> # Important dates in the Nanakshahi calendar
>
> | | |
> |---|---|
> | Guru Gobind Singh's birthday | 5 January |
> | Hola Mohalla | March (date varies) |
> | Vaisakhi | 14 April |
> | Guru Arjan's martyrdom | 16 June |
> | Guru Granth Sahib first installed in Harmandir | 1 September |
> | Bandi Chhor Divas (Divali) | October/November (date varies) |
> | Guru Nanak's birthday | November (date varies) |
> | Guru Tegh Bahadar's martyrdom | 24 November |

Pal Singh Purewal, addressed this situation by devising the Nanakshahi calendar, which is now widely in use among Sikhs.

Acceptance and implementation of the calendar did not go smoothly. In January 2003 an eleven-member committee of Sikhs' principal elected body, the SGPC, ruled that the Panth should no longer calculate its religious anniversaries by the Vikrami calendar but switch to the Nanakshahi calendar. The turbulence prior to the SGPC's approval shows the competing claims to authority of three religious bodies. It also illustrates the inseparability of Sikh political factions from Panthic affairs and the tendency to resolve an impasse by recourse to ordering 'excommunication' of a recalcitrant individual by means of a *hukam-nama*.

The three religious bodies were the Akal Takhat, the SGPC, and the Sant Samaj. The Akal Takhat is the seat of temporal authority which Guru Hargobind established in Amritsar, facing the Harmandir Sahib. It is the Akal Takhat's head, the Jathedar, who is often referred to in English as a high priest or chief priest. In fact, he is not a 'priest' at all (Sikhs have none), but an officer appointed and paid by the SGPC, Sikhs' most powerful elected body. The Sant Samaj (or, to give it its full name, the Gurmat Sidhant Parcharak Sant Samaj) had recently emerged as a coalition of powerful religious leaders, although the prominence of such leaders, the Sants, is nothing new. The Sikh political factions involved in the calendar affair represented competing interests among the Shiromani Akali Dal, the explicitly Sikh party that was founded in 1920.

Pal Singh Purewal's calendar initially met with support from the president of the SGPC, Bibi Jagir Kaur, but with disapproval from the Akal Takhat. Akali politicians backed it, and in December 1999 the Punjab Government announced that Guru Gobind Singh's birthday would be celebrated on the Nanakshahi date of 5 January rather than, in accordance with the older calendar, nine days later. In the event, the Sikh Chief Minister of Punjab, Prakash Singh Badal, was persuaded to agree to the Vikrami date, but the SGPC defiantly went ahead with celebrations on 5 January.

As a result, in January 2000 the Jathedar of Akal Takhat issued a *hukam-nama* (edict) against Bibi Jagir Kaur, excommunicating her from the Panth. In denouncing Bibi Jagir Kaur for authorizing the proposed calendar, the Jathedar had the support of some of the Sant Samaj. The Sants had no wish to concede supremacy to either the SGPC or the Akali Party. However, Bibi Jagir Kaur took no notice of the *hukam-nama*, saying that faxing it from a car was not the way to issue such a decree. Subsequently, members of the SGPC who supported her exercised the SGPC's right to sack the Jathedar and appoint a replacement.

The calendar that eventually received approval in January 2003 from the committee appointed to resolve the problem had been modified (so that the Sant Samaj could accept it) by lessening the gap between the Nanakshahi calendar and the Vikrami calendar. Thus Sikhs' and Hindus' Divali celebrations would continue to coincide, Guru Nanak's birthday would still coincide with the full moon in the lunar month of Kattak and the date of Hola Mohalla would still be one day after the Hindu festival of Holi. However, the name 'Bandi Chhor Divas' ('Release of Prisoners Day') reminds Sikhs of the Panth's specific reason for celebrating what is otherwise a Hindu festival: on Divali day Guru Hargobind left prison, accompanied by prisoners whose release he had negotiated. Guru Gobind Singh's birthday is now celebrated annually on 5 January.

Unquestionably, the Nanakshahi calendar had the advantage that most dates would remain constant by the internationally accepted Gregorian calendar. But a more emotive issue was the extent to which the Panth was, or should be, distinct from Punjabi Hindus. The Akali politicians' backing of the SGPC was in line with their foundational commitment, as Sikhs of a Tat Khalsa persuasion, to the separateness of the Panth. The Vikrami calendar was one of the few elements of Punjab's composite culture to have survived the polarization that the Akalis had set in motion a century earlier. Not only did it mean that Sikhs and Hindus calculated their anniversaries using the same principles but also that they shared major spring and autumn festivities. Establishing a separate calendar defied Hindu tendencies to subsume Sikhism in Hinduism, and it put Sikhs on a par with Hindus, Muslims, and other 'world religions'.

Authority

As the calendar episode shows, controversial institutional issues precipitate acrimonious disputes about where ultimate authority in the Panth resides, and the processes for reaching decisions. Of course, many dilemmas are ethical rather than institutional, and Sikhs need both to know that procedural matters can be resolved responsibly and to whom they can turn for spiritual and moral guidance.

One answer to the question of ultimate authority is that the Guru Granth Sahib provides this, whatever the nature of the quandary.

The 1920 *vak* (see page 119) illustrates the application of this method to social affairs. Political events have also been referred to the Guru Granth Sahib. Thus two *vak*s from the Harmandir Sahib in 1984 were understood by some as the death warrants of the Prime Minister, Indira Gandhi, who had ordered the army assault on the Golden Temple complex.

But, when passages of mystical poetry are employed as an oracle in specific crises, they require interpretation by fallible humans, who may be distraught or predisposed to a particular understanding. What is more, the use of scripture in this way does not always yield a reading that connects with the matter in hand. The question also remains whether a *vak* applies only, or chiefly, to those who consulted the Guru in their specific uncertainty. History does, however, suggest that a *vak* taken in Harmandir Sahib is regarded as particularly weighty and far-reaching.

Whereas the Guru Granth Sahib is not a rule-book, the succession of *rahit-nama*s do provide specific instructions. But these were the product of their time and fail to address some 21st-century issues. Their message aimed at the social segregation of Sikhs and Muslims, as typified by the continuing ban in the Sikh Rahit Maryada on eating halal meat. The current Sikh Rahit Maryada does not, however, perpetuate the earlier hostility. Nonetheless, its concerns do reflect those of late 19th- and early 20th-century Sikh revivalists. Environmental degradation, feminist concerns, and reproductive ethics were not on the agenda in 1951, its year of publication, let alone when it was being formulated between 1928 and 1932. It supports Khalsa-style Sikhi, indicates that authority lies ultimately with the Panth and the Granth, and explains how local *sangat*s should impose a penance for a breach of the Rahit, as well as in what circumstances a Panthic injunction (*gurmata*) should be issued. But its outline of the practical mechanisms for exercising authority and making an appeal contain no indication of how elections should be conducted, or the proper procedure for managing gurdwaras, or even the remit of the Akal Takhat. Issues such as vegetarianism are often decided by individuals' interpretation and the rulings of Sants.

Since the 18th century authority has lain to varying degrees with the Panth as well as with the Granth. But the mechanisms for decision-making, and how extensively the resolutions apply, are a subject of increasing discussion, not least among enquiring diaspora Sikhs.

Discussion hinges in part on the contemporary viability and form of the 18th-century reality of *sarbat khalsa* (the entire Khalsa) and *gurmata* (the Gurus' will). A corporate memory of this procedure survives, as does the authoritative eminence of Akal Takhat, articulated by its Jathedar, or principal officer.

Also up for discussion is how much authority the Akal Takhat and the SGPC have, and how these bodies relate to one another. One key consideration is the fact that the SGPC's remit technically extends only as far as the pre-1966 Indian state of Punjab, in other words it operates only in the present states of Punjab, Haryana, and Himachal Pradesh, but not, for example, in Delhi, let alone the diaspora. Another hotly disputed question is whether only *amritdhari*s are eligible to elect the SGPC. More generally, can only initiated (or, for that matter, only *keshdhari*) Sikhs exercise authority in Sikh congregations worldwide?

In an attempt at resolving the calendar affair in 2000, the Jathedar faxed a *hukam-nama*. Sikhs' opinions of the significance of *hukam-nama*s vary. Currently the Jathedar of Akal Takhat issues a *hukam-nama* in most cases (though not, of course, in the calendar case) on the recommendation of a committee of the SGPC. Bibi Jagir Kaur immediately dismissed the *hukam-nama* directed against her, but so seriously have some individuals taken certain *hukam-nama*s that they felt impelled to take the lives of others. The October 1978 *hukam-nama* ordering the boycott of a particularly controversial group, the Sant Nirankaris, was followed by the killing of their leader. Bloodshed in Canada ensued the 1998 excommunication of Canadian Sikhs for disputing a *hukam-nama* that prohibited the use of chairs and tables in *langar*s in the diaspora. *Hukam-nama*s are often intended to excommunicate, and so isolate, intimidate, or coerce heretics or dissidents.

What troubles some Sikhs is not only uncertainty about the procedures for decision-making and the remit and scope of such decisions, but also the probity of powerful individuals.

Moreover, the predicament of critical scholarship raises the question whether the Panth's leaders are the appropriate authorities for evaluating complex works of scholarship that the detractors of particular academics present to them as heretical writings. In common with the religious authorities of other faiths, the resultant judgements make no allowance for a generic difference between what is appropriate from the pulpit and from the podium.

Another reality is that, as the involvement of the Akali Dal in the calendar affair suggested, faith and politics are inseparable. In the 20th century, one leader, Gurbachan Singh Tohra, was 26 times president of the SGPC, the Panth's highest elected body, as well as being the leader of Shiromani Akali Dal, the powerful Punjab-based political party.

Ethical issues

Sikhs have to tackle ethical challenges as well as to reach decisions about *langar* seating arrangements and the calibration of calendars. Theologians and clergy, whatever their faith, are hard-pressed (and often disunited) as science and technology shift the goalposts of individual choice. Nevertheless, on the analogy of synagogues and churches, it might be assumed that the morally confused Sikh could approach a religious professional in the local gurdwara. But the lay character of the Panth means that there is no comparable body of clergy who have been trained in answering theological and ethical questions.

This situation is compounded for Sikhs in the diaspora, as the *granthi*s and *giani*s are in many cases recent arrivals from Punjab, with little grasp of their *sangat*'s social context. The greater ease of diaspora-born Sikhs in the local vernacular (usually English) than in Punjabi makes discussion of ethical dilemmas even less feasible, and fear of gossip within the community also discourages openness. The challenges of social change and scientific advance in the 20th and 21st centuries, and the stimulus from inter-faith discussions and (in the UK) multi-faith religious education syllabuses, may further motivate Sikh writers to formulate Sikh responses to issues such as homosexuality, genetic engineering, human cloning, surrogacy, and the use of embryos in medical research, as well as debating the ethics of nuclear war.

As Chapter 7 has shown, there are contemporary issues on which a religiously informed Sikh position would be a straightforward development of the Gurus' explicit prohibition. The abortion of unwanted daughters is one example. Smoking is another, and verses in the Guru Granth Sahib unambiguously rule out befuddling the senses with alcohol, and so, by extension, with narcotics. The 21st century's greater challenge for Sikhs is to resist social pressure, exerted within their families. The expectations that the bride's family will lay on impressively generous supplies of alcoholic drinks for wedding guests, and the encouragement of pregnant women to misuse medical facilities in order to avoid having daughters, exemplify powerful pressures in Punjabi society.

An area in which Guru Gobind Singh gave a clear lead is that of war and peace. In the Zafarnama, a letter to the Mughal emperor, he wrote:

> When all efforts to restore peace prove useless and no words avail
> Lawful is the flash of steel, it is right to draw the sword.

But how quickly this last resort arrives is open to disagreement. The ideal of the *sant sipahi* stresses spiritual stamina as much as military force, and the early 20th-century Akalis exemplified the courage of non-violent protest. The potential scale of 21st-century conflicts raises questions that religious leaders have not previously faced.

Challenges to traditional authority

Meanwhile, the increasing influence of overseas Sikh communities looks set to disturb the institutional authorities in Amritsar. In this process the rapid uptake of information technology is playing a part. Mistrust of Sikh institutions coincides with increasing recourse by Sikhs, especially younger Sikhs, to the internet. The Canadian scholar Doris Jakobsh poses the question: are the creators of the many websites that are devoted to Sikhism in fact the new authorities of Sikhism? It is on the internet that increasing numbers of Sikhs feel confident to voice uncertainties and to offer advice, finding in the process a sense of community. By 2004, there were over 1,800 Sikh websites and an estimated 200 Sikh discussion groups. These provide a transnational forum for exchanging news and debating contentious issues in relation to the Gurus' teaching and the Panth's experience. The internet provides easy access to the sacred text of the Guru Granth Sahib and virtual visits to the Harmandir Sahib and other holy sites, and it offers information. What is sometimes less easy to ascertain is the reliability and stance of various sources to which the internet lends a spurious authority. Thanks to the World Wide Web, questing and scattered Sikhs find the support of a virtual *sangat*: discussion groups bring together like-minded Sikhs who share anxieties, discoveries, and spiritual insights, and often reinforce their political positions.

Sikhism: the emergence of a religion

Sikhism's standing in relation to other faith communities is a recurrent theme of Sikh discourse. Article 25 of India's constitution, promulgated in 1950, fuels Sikhs' long-running campaign for its revision, because it refers to Sikhs, along with Buddhists and Jains, as Hindus. The calendar initiative and its setbacks came in a long line of debates spotlighting the uneasy relationship between the Panth and Hindu tradition. Historically, the inescapable context of Sikhi is Hindu, at least in its widest sense of Indic. The substratum for Sikh philosophical and cultural expression, and its idiom, is in this broad sense Hindu.

The ways in which Indic tradition provides a repertoire include the customs of some minorities, whether members of particular caste groups or followers of particular Sants. Among these are some Bhatras' domestic worship on Divali day and some Ramgarhias' veneration, on the following day, of their tools in front of a representation of Brahma's son, Vishvakarma, the architect of the cosmos. Similarly, the elaborate attention to the Guru Granth Sahib in Nanaksar gurdwaras echoes details of veneration in Hindu shrines. The rule that *bahingam*s in Nanaksar gurdwaras should observe celibacy comes not from Sikh roots, but from Hindu concerns about purity. Similarly, the Akhand Kirtani Jatha's avoidance of eating with other Sikhs parallels the taboos on dining together that Hindu castes have observed.

Indic norms frame 'mainstream' Sikh practice too. The bathing of the *nishan sahib* flagstaff outside gurdwaras in dilute yoghurt on Vaisakhi day, and the use of milk for the daily washing of the marble platform around Harmandir Sahib, are consistent with Hindu regard for the cow, whose milk is seen to be both pure and purificatory. If we shift from ritual cleansing today to Guru Gobind Singh's poetic understanding of his distinctive Khalsa, we find that the Dasam Granth situates it in a Hindu narrative. Guru Gobind

Singh is, in this interpretation, setting his project in the age-old mythic confrontation between the forces of good and evil, between the Goddess and the demons.

What is certain is that, at different junctures, individuals and groups consciously rejected aspects of the religious and cultural practices of both Hindus and Muslims. Thus Guru Nanak rejected image-worship, Guru Gobind Singh's *rahit* marked his Khalsa out as distinct in their social conventions from Muslims, the Tat Khalsa ruled out the use of Hindu rites, and the Akalis removed the *mahant*s.

To move on to the suggestion in Chapter 1 that Sikhism is a distinct revelation: the immediacy of Guru Nanak's religious experience and message leaves no doubt of his own sense of exceptional vocation. Moreover, the basis of a strong Panth was laid by Guru Nanak himself through his *shabad*s and his development of the Kartarpur community, moulding and inaugurating community institutions. The Bachittar Natak, one of Guru Gobind Singh's poems in the Dasam Granth, presents him, too, as a leader with a God-given mission. But using the primarily Christian language of 'revelation' may well imply a separateness from the Sants, Kabir and Ravidas, that the Gurus did not feel or intend. Sikhi in its entirety evolved during the Guru period and beyond, but emphasis on revelation obscures this aspect of development over time.

As for being a 'separate nation', beyond doubt Sikhs constitute a *qaum*, in the sense of a cohesive people, and have regarded themselves as such since the middle of the 19th century. But is this the same as a nation? And does nationhood imply the need for a state? The goal of nationhood had its roots in European history, which, in the 19th century, suggested that nationalism grows as religion weakens its hold on the popular imagination. Nevertheless, the 20th century saw religion's grip strengthening in many societies and the formation of nation states that were defined by Islam. The

Partition in 1947 of the Sikhs' homeland, Punjab, had given Muslim Punjabis an Islamic state, Pakistan, while Hindu and Sikh Punjabis were nationals of the new secular, but Hindu-majority, state of India.

'*Raj karega Khalsa*' ('The Khalsa shall rule') is the Sikh affirmation at the end of the Ardas, and it can be understood spiritually and metaphorically or more literally. (It also provided one newspaper,

21. India's first Sikh prime minister, Manmohan Singh, after being sworn into office in May 2004. Since 1947 political relations between Sikhs and the Indian state have been a significant element in Sikh history

The Asian Age, with a whimsical headline on 20 May 2004 when Dr Manmohan Singh had agreed to become India's fourteenth prime minister, the first Sikh to hold this office.) Historically, the slogans '*Raj karega Khalsa*' and '*Sri Vahiguruji ki Fateh*' ('Victory is God's') have fired Sikhs' sense of future sovereignty.

In addition to the energetic campaigning by Sikhs in Punjab and in the diaspora for Khalistan, it is salutary to note not only the contribution of diaspora Sikhs in the 1980s and 1990s, but also the part played earlier by the British in providing and sustaining the rhetoric of Sikh nationhood. Cunningham's history of 1849 described Guru Nanak as:

> perceiv[ing] the true principles of reform, and ... lay[ing] those broad foundations which enabled his successor Guru Gobind Singh to fire the minds of his countrymen with a new nationality.

The British Law Lords' more cautiously worded ruling in 1983 that Sikhs are 'almost a nation' made much of the concept of ethnicity. Certainly, Sikhs are a group seen by themselves and others as a distinct community, with a shared history of which the group is conscious and the memory of which it keeps alive, and with a social tradition of its own. But arguing that Sikhs are ethnically distinct from other Punjabis will remain problematic, especially for Hindu Punjabis. As a result of the Law Lords' ruling, religious discrimination against Sikhs in the UK is covered by Race Relations legislation. Whether or not the Panth is a nation is for each reader to decide.

Amid the debates, the case for Sikhism as a religion is secure thanks to its inspirational 'founders', sacred certainties, and its much-revered scripture, its distinctive life-cycle rites and festivals. Sikhs have places of congregational worship and sites hallowed by pilgrimage. The Panth has organizational structures and religious authorities. The fact that the authority of certain bodies is strongly contested, and that there is no tidy, centralized hierarchy, demonstrates the Panth's vitality rather than either its imminent demise or that it fails to meet arbitrary criteria for being a fully fledged 'religion'. Sikhs share pride in the reign of Maharaja Ranjit Singh and in generations of military prowess, and anguish at the rupture of their homeland in 1947 and at the desecration of Harmandir Sahib in 1984. Martyrdom (*shahidi*) is a recurrent experience, strongly marking out Sikh consciousness from Hindu. Enthusiastic celebration of historic anniversaries on a bigger and bigger scale is another hallmark of the Panth.

At the same time, a full understanding of Sikhi, of the Gurbani and the Khalsa *rahit*, requires knowledge of other streams of Indian religious tradition and history, and especially of their cross-currents in the Punjab. The Panth has 'fuzzy' edges, and it is internally diverse and changing. These facts exemplify the blurred boundaries and interpenetration, in different ways, of faith traditions and faith communities, including 'world religions', in general. For world religions are intrinsically complex and diverse, whatever their spokespersons' aspirations to uniformity and unity. In the Sikh case, this diversity is evident not only in the twist and hue of turbans but also in liturgy, including the procedures for administering *amrit* in the initiation rite of *khande di pahul*. The 21st century, with the advantages of virtual networking in cyberspace, may well foster minority groups.

Simultaneously, Sikhs' tendency to speak of 'our Bible', of 'priests', and even 'high priests', and of 'baptism' combine to erode Sikhism's distinctiveness. By calling the Guru Granth Sahib 'our bible', Sikhs obscure their scripture's status as living Guru. Those who refer to *granthi*s as priests and to *jathedar*s at the Akal Takhat, Amritsar, as 'high priests' do a disservice to a proudly lay tradition. (The term *jathedar* has the meaning of leader of a military detachment, or 'captain'.) It is important that Sikhs affirm, and that non-Sikhs come to realize, the Gurus' emphasis on a path of *bhakti* and *seva*, unmediated by priests. Neither *granthi* nor *jathedar* is a priest by virtue of either ordination (as in Christian tradition) or birth (unlike members of the Hindus' Brahmin caste). There are no close Sikh counterparts of the Christians' and Jews' seminaries or theological colleges, which provide training in theology and pastoral care. Sikhs' use of the word 'baptism' for *amrit chhakana* (a usage to be found at least as early as Max Arthur Macauliffe's influential *The Sikh Religion*) also cries out for comment. Both *amrit sanskar* and (Christian) baptism require water, and both rites mark a transition, but the differences are no less significant. The use of 'excommunication' for *tanakhah*, the penance imposed on a Khalsa Sikh for violating the *rahit*, is another instance. In the interests of accuracy, the practitioners of a 'separate religion' need to use with confidence, and with due explanation, the terminology of Sikhi, and to be clear about aspects of the Panth's distinctiveness which the English words mask.

Contemporary Sikhs' application to their own distinctive institutions of English terms, which have been honed in another faith tradition, is consistent with the Singh Sabha reformers' appropriation of 'God' and 'monotheism' at the turn of the 20th century. Any weakening of conceptual boundaries may be welcomed as evidence of convergence between previously independent communities. While English words, such as 'God' and 'baptism', are gaining a wider range of meaning, those who are concerned to understand Gurmat and the Panth need to be critically aware of ongoing processes of social and linguistic adaptation.

Over the past century, the terms 'world religion' and 'world faith' have become increasingly current in literature about religion. In the UK, where the Sikh community is outnumbered only by Christians, Muslims, and Hindus, Sikhism features in schools' religious education syllabuses as one of the six 'principal religions'. Sikhism is a 'world religion' not only in the sense that Sikhs now live in substantial numbers in all the inhabited continents, but also in the sense that the Gurus' insights potentially provide challenge

22. 'For last six miles I run while talking to God', the words of 93-year-old Fauja Singh, a 21st-century exemplar of the Sikh emphasis on *nam simaran*, physical discipline, and voluntary service (*seva*). In his 90s, Fauja Singh ran marathons in London, New York, and Toronto to raise money for charities

and comfort for people of every background. Increasingly, with the self-assurance of a world faith, the Panth may welcome that rigorous scholarly attention to which all world religions are exposed, rather than reacting defensively with cries of an endangered Panth, with calumny, boycott, and the imposition of penance on Sikh scholars.

The subject of spirituality, elusively challenging attempts at definition, attracts increasing attention across a widening vista of academic disciplines and types of organization. Spirituality, in the sense of human questing and experience at depth, and of individual health and community well-being infused by transcendent or universal meaning, is no longer tied to specific religious faiths. At the same time, for the person of religious faith, spirituality and religion are mutually nurturing and integrally related.

Guru Nanak's emphasis on integrity, and an inner focus upon divine truth, rather than upon religions' trappings, provides a basis for spiritual development far beyond the Khalsa, or indeed the Panth. Similarly, at the heart of Sikhi are principles that can contribute strongly to inter-faith dialogue. Whereas isolation and conversion had characterized relations in previous centuries, increasing globalization challenged religious adherents to seek practical cooperation for the common good, based upon deepening mutual understanding. To this ongoing endeavour Sikhi has the potential to contribute from its principles of respecting spiritual paths while retaining its focus on God the True Guru.

In conclusion

Marriage provides a metaphor for concluding this Very Short Introduction to Sikhism. As we have seen, the view of Sikhism as a marrying together of elements of the older faiths of Hinduism and Islam misleadingly oversimplifies the development of the Sikh community and of the Sikh tradition. It cannot be written off as a (mere) syncretism.

To continue the metaphor of union, from within the Sikh tradition come compellingly brief formulae, pairings of terms, which encapsulate Sikhi. We have seen Guru Hargobind's principle of *miri* combined with *piri*, the concepts of the temporal and the spiritual, united. This coupling was symbolized by his own two swords and continues in the pair of swords which cup the rest of the Khalsa emblem, the *khanda*. Similarly, the cry '*degh tegh fateh*' (victory to the cooking pot and to the sword) summed up the combined emphasis on military readiness to fight oppression and on the ready hospitality of the shared *langar* meal. Then there is that striking union between the life of contemplation and military preparedness as a *sant sipahi*.

Staying with the metaphor of marriage (or perhaps of the spreading out of family members) we can also think of that most creative of contemporary relationships – the relationship between Sikhs in India and Sikhs outside India. Clearly, how Sikhs and their institutional bodies in Punjab relate to Sikhs overseas, especially in North America and the UK, is crucial to the community's evolution

23. *Ragis* (musicians) playing *tabla* (drums) and harmonium in the gurdwara

and to intellectually coherent articulations of the faith in the face of the 21st century's successive challenges.

These will continue to provide opportunities to test the unlikely union on which Sikhism is founded, a volume of unsettling, inspirational insights expressed in mystical poetry embraced as Guru by a vigorous, versatile populace with a warrior image and ideal. And, at the heart of the Gurus' outpouring is the union of the yearning human soul with its divine bridegroom. This is the union to which individual Sikhs daily aspire as they hear and repeat the name of their beloved, whose *nam* is Truth.

Meanwhile, Khalsa Sikhs' faithfulness to their proud and vulnerable visibility will continue to bring Sikhi to the attention of spiritual questers and intellectual questioners. In turn, they too will discover the spiritual and physical nourishment of *kirtan* and *langar*, and will ponder the call to conspicuous and costly loyalty.

Further reading

General introductions

W. O. Cole, *Understanding Sikhism* (Edinburgh: Dunedin Academic Press, 2004)

W. O. Cole and P. S. Sambhi, *The Sikhs: Their Religious Beliefs and Practices* (Brighton: Sussex Academic Press, 1995)

S. S. Kalsi, *Simple Guide to Sikhism* (Folkestone: Global Books, 1999)

G. S. Mann, *Sikhism* (Upper Saddle River, NJ: Prentice Hall, 2004)

W. H. McLeod, *Sikhism* (London: Penguin, 1997)

C. Shackle, 'Sikhism', in *Religions in the Modern World*, ed. L. Woodhead, P. Fletcher, H. Kawanami, and D. Smith (London: Routledge, 2002), pp. 70–85

Reference works

W. H. McLeod, *Historical Dictionary of Sikhism* (Lanham, Md, and London: The Scarecrow Press, 1995)

Harbans Singh (ed.), *The Encyclopaedia of Sikhism*, 4 vols (Patiala: Punjabi University, 1995–8)

Scriptures: complete text

For the text in Gurmukhi, with a translation in modern Punjabi, *www.gurugranthdarpan.com/* 0010.html. An English rendering is available at the time of publication at *www.srigranth.org/about.html*, which also provides the Gurmukhi text and its transcription into the Roman and Devanagri scripts.

Scriptures: selections

C. K. Ajit Singh, *The Wisdom of Sikhism* (Oxford: Oneworld, 2001)

Max Arthur Macauliffe, *The Sikh Religion* (New Delhi: S. Chand and Co., 1963)

W. H. McLeod, *Textual Sources for the Study of Sikhism* (Chicago: University of Chicago Press, 1990)

Nikky-Guninder Kaur Singh, *The Name of My Beloved: Verses of the Sikh Gurus* (San Francisco: Harper San Francisco, 1996)

Trilochan Singh, Jodh Singh, Kapur Singh, Harkishen Singh, and Khushwant Singh (ed. and tr.), *Selections from the Sacred Writings of the Sikhs* (London: Allen and Unwin, 1960)

Religious texts

Jodh Singh, *Varan Bhai Gurdas: Text, Transliteration and Translation*, vols 1 and 2 (Patiala and New Delhi: Vision and Venture, 1998)

—— and Dharam Singh, *Sri Dasam Granth Sahib: Text and Translation*, vols 1 and 2 (Patiala: Heritage Publications, 1999)

Textual studies

G. S. Mann, *The Making of Sikh Scripture* (New Delhi: Oxford University Press, 2001)

Pashaura Singh, *The Guru Granth Sahib: Canon, Meaning and Authority* (New Delhi: Oxford University Press, 2000)

—— *The Bhagats of the Guru Granth Sahib: Sikh Self-Definition and the Bhagat Bani* (New Delhi: Oxford University Press, 2003)

History: general

J. S. Grewal, *The New Cambridge History of India*: II.3 *The Sikhs of the Punjab* (Cambridge: Cambridge University Press, 1990)

W. H. McLeod, *Sikhs and Sikhism* (New Delhi: Oxford University Press, 1999)

Khushwant Singh, *A History of the Sikhs*, vols 1 and 2 (New Delhi: Oxford University Press, 1999)

18th and 19th centuries

L. E. Fenech, *Martyrdom in the Sikh Tradition: Playing the 'Game of Love'* (New Delhi: Oxford University Press, 2000)

W. H. McLeod, *Sikhs of the Khalsa: A History of the Khalsa Rahit* (New Delhi: Oxford University Press, 2003)

H. S. Oberoi, *The Construction of Religious Boundaries: Culture, Identity and Diversity in the Sikh Tradition* (New Delhi: Oxford University Press, 1994)

20th century and diaspora

T. S. Bains and H. Johnston, *The Four Quarters of the Night: The Life-Journey of an Emigrant Sikh* (Montreal and Kingston: McGill-Queen's University Press, 1995)

N. G. Barrier and Verne A. Dusenbery (eds.), *The Sikh Diaspora: Migration and Experience beyond Punjab* (Delhi: Chanakya Publications, 1989)

J. S. Grewal, *Contesting Interpretations of the Sikh Tradition* (Delhi: Manohar, 1998)

A. W. Helweg, *Sikhs in England*, 2nd edn. (New Delhi: Oxford University Press, 1986)

Patwant Singh and H. K. Sekhon, *Garland Round my Neck: The Story of Puran Singh of Pingalwara* (New Delhi: UBS Publishers, 2001)

D. S. Tatla, *The Sikh Diaspora: The Search for Statehood* (London: UCL Press, 1999)

Caste and gender

D. Jakobsh, *Relocating Gender in Sikh History: Transformation, Meaning and Identity* (New Delhi: Oxford University Press, 2003)

S. S. Kalsi, *The Evolution of a Sikh Community in Britain* (Leeds: Community Religions Project, Department of Theology and Religious Studies, University of Leeds, 1992)

W. H. McLeod, 'Caste in the Sikh Panth', in W. H. McLeod, *Sikhs and Sikhism* (New Delhi: Oxford University Press, 1999)

S. K. Rait, *Sikh Women in England: Religious, Social and Cultural Beliefs* (Stoke on Trent: Trentham Books, 2005)

Nikky-Guninder Kaur Singh, *The Feminine Principle in the Sikh Vision of the Transcendent* (Cambridge: Cambridge University Press, 1993)

Journals

International Journal of Punjab Studies, 1994–2003
Journal of Punjab Studies, 2004–
Journal of Sikh Studies, 1974–
Sikh Formations: Religion, Culture and Theory, 2005–

Glossary

Punj = Punjabi; Skt = Sanskrit

Adi Granth: Guru Granth Sahib, scripture

ahankar: pride

Akal Takhat: building facing Darbar Sahib, Sikhs' seat of religious authority

Akali: early 20th-century movement for Sikh reform; from the 20th century, a Sikh political party

Akhand Kirtani Jatha: movement of Khalsa Sikhs inspired by Bhai Randhir Singh

akhand path: uninterrupted 48-hour-long reading of Guru Granth Sahib

amrit: literally, 'non-death', water of immortality, nectar; water used in *amrit sanskar*

amrit sanskar: initiation to Khalsa

amrit vela: period before dawn favoured for meditation

amritdhari: initiated Sikh

Ardas: congregational prayer or petition

avatar: 'descent', incarnation of God (in Hindu tradition)

bani: utterance

bhai: brother; respectful title for a man

bhagat: a devotee, in particular the saint-poets, such as Kabir and Namdev

bhagat bani: compositions by the *bhagat*s in the scriptures

bhakti: devotion

bhangra: Punjabi folk-dance; modern music or dance derived from this

Bhatra: first *zat* to settle in the United Kingdom

Bikrami: *see* Vikrami

bir: volume, recension

Chamar: *zat* associated with skinning and tanning

chaur(i): symbol of Guru Granth Sahib's authority, a 'whisk' made of white horse or yak hair

chunni: lightweight long scarf, worn with *salvar kamiz*

dal: cooked lentils

Darbar Sahib: 'revered royal court', the Golden Temple or Harmandir Sahib in Amritsar, Sikhs' most honoured shrine

dharma (Skt); **dharam** (Punj): appropriate behaviour, righteousness, 'religion'

dharamsala: resting place for pilgrims; former term for a *gurdwara*

Five Ks: outward marks of a Khalsa Sikh

giani: literally 'learned', an officiant in a gurdwara

Golden Temple: *see* Darbar Sahib

granth: (pron. 'grunt') volume of scripture

granthi: attendant on Guru Granth Sahib

gurbani: Guru Granth Sahib

gurdwara: Sikh place of worship

Gurmat: Guru's doctrine, Sikhism

gurmata: literally 'will of the Guru'; decision of the gathered Khalsa

gurmukh: devout Sikh

Gurmukhi: script of the Sikh scriptures

gurpurab: religious anniversary, for example the birth of a Guru

Guru Granth Sahib: Sikh scripture

gutka: religious handbook

haumai: ego

Harmandir Sahib: *see* Darbar Sahib

hukam-nama: (1) edict from Guru or from Akal Takhat; (2) = *vak*

izzat: family honour

ik oankar: God is one; opening statement of *mul mantar*; a Sikh logo

janam-sakhi: literally 'birth witness'; collection of traditional stories of Guru Nanak's life.

japan: (pron. jup-un), to repeat, that is in remembrance of *nam*

Japji: Guru Nanak's hymn at start of Guru Granth Sahib

Jat: Sikhs' largest *zat*, a hereditary land-owning community

jati: endogamous caste group = *zat*

jatha: military detachment; name for some Sikh organizations

jathedar: leader, head of Akal Takhat

kachh, kachhahira: cotton breeches, one of the Five Ks

kam: lust

kangha: small wooden comb, one of the Five Ks

kara: iron or steel circle worn round the wrist as a 'bangle', one of the Five Ks

karah prashad: sweet made of flour, sugar, butter, and water, distributed at religious gatherings

karma (Skt.); **karam** (Punj): the law of moral cause and effect

kesh: uncut hair; one of the Five Ks

keshdhari: Sikh who does not shave or shorten his/her hair

keski: small turban worn by women in Akhand Kirtani Jatha

Khalsa: literally 'pure', 'owing allegiance to no intermediary'; Sikh(s), esp. *amritdhari* Sikh(s)

khanda: double-edged sword; Khalsa symbol which includes *khanda*

khande di pahul: = *amrit sanskar*

Khatri: a caste associated with book-keeping

khir: sweet rice pudding

kirpan: sword, one of the Five Ks (the vowels are pronounced like those of 'Iran')

kirtan: singing of *shabad*s (the vowels are like those in 'key' and 'ton')

krodh: anger

kurahit: prohibition

langar: shared vegetarian meal prepared and eaten in gurdwara; the kitchen/canteen area of the gurdwara

lobh: craving

mahant: until early 20th century, custodian of historic gurdwaras

man: (rhymes with 'ton') mind, capriciousness

manji: administrative area from time of Guru Amar Das

manmukh: self-willed individual

masand: agent responsible for a *manji*

maya: delusion, false priorities

mazhab: religion

mela: literally 'fair'; festival, for example Divali (but not used for *gurpurabs*)

miri: temporal authority

misal: literally 'file'; 18th-century band of Sikh warriors

moh: materialism

moksha (Skt); *mukti* (Punj): release from being reborn

Mughal: Muslim dynasty ruling in North India from 1526

mul mantar: Guru Nanak's statement with which Guru Granth Sahib commences

nam: literally 'name'; central Sikh concept; divine reality

Namdhari: a reform movement prominent in the 19th century

Nath: (rhymes with 'part') title for devotees of (Hindu) god Shiva

Nihang: Sikh preserving an 18th-century warrior tradition

Nirankari: a reform movement emphasizing God as formless (*nirankar*)

nirgun: literally 'without qualities', formless (title of God)

nishan sahib: Sikh pennant bearing *khanda* emblem of Khalsa

nitnem: daily prayer

oankar: *see ik oankar*

Om: sound/syllable representing ultimate reality (in Hindu tradition)

palki: stand supporting Guru Granth Sahib

pandit: Brahmin, Hindu priest

panj: five

panjabiat: Punjabi culture

Panth: (pron. 'punt') Sikh community

Paramatma: cosmic soul, God

path: (pron. 'part') reading of scripture

patit: lapsed (from Khalsa discipline)

piri: spiritual authority

pothi: (pron. 'poe-tee') book, specifically compilation of Gurus' hymns

qaum: (pron 'cowm') people, community, 'nation'

rag: raga, musical mode

ragi: musician

rahit: discipline

rahit-nama: code of Sikh discipline

Ramgarhia: *zat* traditionally employed in construction

rumala: cloth covering Guru Granth Sahib when not being read

sach-khand: ultimate stage of spiritual progression; night-time resting place for Guru Granth Sahib

sadhsangat: righteous congregation

sagun: 'possessing qualities'; God as conceived of with attributes

sahajdhari: literally 'slow adopter', non-*keshdhari* Sikh

salvar kamiz: Punjabi suit, worn by many Sikh women

sampradaya: (usually Hindu) grouping revering a succession of gurus

sanatan: term applied to Sikhs with an inclusive attitude towards Hindu tradition

sangat: congregation

Sant: medieval poet-mystics; title for some 20th- and 21st-century spiritual and political leaders

sardar(ji): chief, title for Sikh male

Satguru: true Guru, God

Satnam: whose name is Truth (that is, God)

seva: voluntary service, a key principle of Sikhi

SGPC: Shiromani Gurdwara Parbandhak Committee, Sikhs' most powerful elected body

shabad: word, composition in the Guru Granth Sahib, 'hymn'

shahid: martyr

Sikhi: Gurus' teaching, Sikhism

Sikh Rahit Maryada: Code of Discipline, published in 1950

simaran: 'to remember', that is, remembrance of *nam*, meditation

Singh Sabha: movement of Sikh renewal beginning in late 19th century

Tat Khalsa: (1) after Guru Gobind Singh's death, Sikhs who did not follow Banda; (2) late 19th-century/early 20th-century reformist Sikhs critical of *sanatan* Sikhs

tirath: (pronounced 'tee-rut') place of pilgrimage

Udasi: ascetic movement associated with Guru Nanak's son Siri Chand

Vahiguru: God

vak: random reading from Guru Granth Sahib for spiritual guidance

var: praise-poem

varna (Skt); ***varan*** (Punj): hereditary 'class' in four-tier social
hierarchy

Vikrami: a Hindu calendar

zat: caste, *jati*

Timeline

1173–1266	Life of Farid, a Sufi whose compositions are the earliest material in the Guru Granth Sahib.
1469	Birth of Guru Nanak, the first Guru.
1539	Guru Angad becomes the second Guru.
1552	Guru Amar Das becomes the third Guru.
1574	Guru Ram Das becomes the fourth Guru.
1581	Guru Arjan Dev becomes the fifth Guru.
1604	Installation of the scriptures in Harmandir Sahib, Amritsar.
1606	Martyrdom of Guru Arjan Dev. Guru Hargobind becomes the sixth Guru.
1644	Guru Har Rai becomes the seventh Guru.
1661	Guru Har Krishan becomes the eighth Guru.
1664	Guru Tegh Bahadur becomes the ninth Guru.
1675	Guru Tegh Bahadur is martyred and Gobind Singh becomes the tenth Guru.
1699	Guru Gobind Singh initiates the Khalsa.
1708	Death of Guru Gobind Singh, ending of line of human Gurus.
1799–1839	Maharaja Ranjit Singh's reign over Punjab.

1845–1846	First Anglo-Sikh War
1848–1849	Second Anglo-Sikh War
1849	British annexation of Punjab.
1873	The first Singh Sabha is founded in Amritsar.
1907	First gurdwara in Canada.
1909	The Anand Marriage Act recognizes the Sikh rite.
1911	First gurdwara in the United Kingdom.
1912	First gurdwara in the United States of America.
1920	The Akali Party is established to free gurdwaras in Punjab from corrupt management. The Shiromani Gurdwara Parbandhak Committee (SGPC) is founded.
1925	The Sikh Gurdwaras Act confers control of Punjab's historic gurdwaras on the SGPC.
1947	India gains independence from Britain. Punjab is divided between India and the newly created state of Pakistan. Sikhs flee to India.
1950	The Rahit Maryada, a definitive code of Khalsa Sikh discipline, is published.
1966	Indian state of Punjab is subdivided. The new Punjab is India's first Sikh majority state.
c. 1970	Sikhs leave East Africa to settle mainly in the United Kingdom.
1982	Giani Zail Singh becomes the first Sikh president of India.
1984	Indian army's assault on the Akal Takht in the Harmandir Sahib complex and the death of the militant Sikh preacher Jarnail Singh Bhindranwale.
2003	Calendar reform: the Nanakshahi calendar comes into use.
2004	Manmohan Singh is elected the first Sikh prime minister of India.

Index

Index

Expand your collection of
VERY SHORT INTRODUCTIONS